YORK NOTES

General Editors: Professor A.N. Jeffares (University of Stirling) & Professor Suheil Bushrui (American University of Beirut)

Homer

THE ILIAD

Notes by Robin Sowerby

MA PH D (CAMBRIDGE)
Lecturer, Department of English Studies, University of Stirling

LONGMAN
YORK PRESS

YORK PRESS
Immeuble Esseily, Place Riad Solh, Beirut.

LONGMAN GROUP UK LIMITED
Longman House, Burnt Mill, Harlow,
Essex CM20 2JE, England
Associated companies, branches and representatives
throughout the world

First published 1985
Third impression 1991

ISBN 0-582-79227-4

Produced by Longman Group (FE) Ltd.
Printed in Hong Kong

Contents

Part 1

Introduction

The 'Homeric question'

Nothing is known for certain about the authorship of the *Iliad* or about its date and place of composition. Indeed all the circumstances surrounding the composition and early transmission of the Homeric poems are matters of surmise and controversy that together have come to be known as the 'Homeric question'. It is unlikely that a satisfactory solution to the problem that has greatly perplexed scholars and critics alike for nearly two centuries will ever now be found. The literature upon the subject is very considerable and all that can be done here is to indicate some of the main difficulties and to record the latest consensus of scholarly opinion. That consensus may be more apparent than real and at best can only offer a likely theory.

The *Iliad* and the *Odyssey* are the oldest surviving texts in Greek literature. There are no internal references to their author or to their origin and there are no other contemporary documents to throw light upon them. They exist in what is virtually an historical vacuum. Nor is there any reliable tradition about their origin in the earliest Greek literature following them. The Greeks all agree on the name 'Homer' and there is a persistent tradition that like the bard Demodocus in the *Odyssey* he was blind, but different views are recorded concerning his date and birthplace. Seven cities claimed to be the birthplace of Homer, the most favoured in antiquity being Chios and Smyrna, both in the region of Ionia in the eastern Aegean. The Greeks believed in the historical reality of the Trojan War, but the reliability of the Homeric version was questioned. According to some accounts he was a contemporary witness of events; according to others his poem was composed some time after the fall of Troy, an event which in any case was for the earliest Greek historians shrouded in the mists of pre-history.

Any consideration of the Homeric question must begin with the picture of the Homeric bard in the *Odyssey*. There are two bards in the poem, Phemius, resident in the palace of Odysseus in Ithaca, and the blind Demodocus who resides in the palace of King Alcinous in Phaeacia which is visited by Odysseus in the course of his wanderings from Troy. Both bards have an honoured place and sing to the accompaniment of the lyre. Phemius sings of the woes inflicted on the

Greeks returning from Troy (I, 326–7). Demodocus sings three short songs, the first of which is about a quarrel between the leading Greeks at the beginning of the Trojan story (VIII, 73–82). The second is a comic tale about the gods (VIII, 266–366). The third is at the request of Odysseus, who commends Demodocus for his truthfulness in faithfully recording the memory of the sufferings of the Greeks at Troy and asks him to sing of the Wooden Horse, the stratagem by which the Greeks took Troy. Demodocus, stirred by the god of song, begins from the point at which the Greeks sailed away (line 500). He tells how the Trojans took the huge horse into the city thinking that the Greeks had departed, and how the Greeks hidden inside it came out at night and sacked the city (VIII, 487–520). The implication is that Demodocus knows many songs about gods and heroes and that in particular he knows the whole Trojan story which he can take up at any point. Moreover it is implied that the bard transmits faithfully the memory of the great events of the past. Later in the poem Phemius boasts to Odysseus that he is self-taught and knows many different songs. The poet of the *Iliad* and *Odyssey* must be a literary descendant of the Homeric bard as he appears in the *Odyssey*. But Demodocus and Phemius work on a small scale, reciting single tales. There is no hint in either the *Iliad* or the *Odyssey* of an occasion which could have prompted the composition of poems of such great length and scope.

How could the poems have been transmitted? Early literary sources report the existence of a guild called the Homeridae who, claiming to be the descendants of Homer, flourished in Chios and were devoted to the recitation of his poems. In addition there were other professional reciters of Homer's poetry called rhapsodes. Their existence is well attested, and they recited Homer's poetry from memory at public festivals and games where they competed with one another for prizes. Again it is difficult to imagine an occasion on which the poems might have been recited in their entirety.

It was the lack of any known occasion for the composition of poems of this length, together with the difficulty of explaining how poems of this length and artistic unity could have been composed without the aid of writing, that led the German Homeric scholar Friedrich Wolf (1759–1824) to raise the Homeric question. It is not that Wolf denied the existence of 'Homer'. He believed that Homer had existed and had initiated the poems in their early form. But he declared in his *Prolegomena ad Homerum* of 1795 that the Homeric poems as we know them did not have a single author but had progressively evolved as successive rhapsodes added and developed what had come down to them. Some ancient scholars known as the chorizontes or separators had believed that the *Iliad* and the *Odyssey* were by different authors, and some ancient commentators had suspected that particular lines and even some episodes had been interpolated, but it was not until Wolf that unity of authorship of the individual poems was fundamentally questioned.

Wolf's theory arose primarily from a consideration of the external factors mentioned above. After him the poems themselves were rigorously analysed. Internal discrepancies and inconsistencies were seen to be evidence of multiple authorship. During this time even those who disagreed with Wolf's conclusions accepted that the *Iliad* and *Odyssey* had come into being gradually over a period of time, since it is apparent that like a rock face they contain various layers of material some of which must be given a comparatively late date while others belong to earlier time.

Archaeology and the *Iliad*

The ancient Greeks had believed in the substantial reality of Homer's world but in modern times students of Homer from the eighteenth century onwards tended to believe that the material world of Homer and the events he described were poetic fictions, until in the later part of the nineteenth century archaeologists began to reconstruct the early history of civilisation in the Mediterranean from the physical evidence provided by excavations. The most famous name in Homeric archaeology is that of the German scholar Heinrich Schliemann (1822–90) who excavated what he believed to be the site of Troy at Hissarlik in northern Turkey in the early 1870s. His conviction that he had found Homer's Troy has been vindicated by all the subsequent research into the evidence. He later excavated Mycenae (1876) and Tiryns (1884) on the Greek mainland. Other places mentioned in Homer, notably Pylos, were investigated by other archaeologists. Shortly after 1900 Sir Arthur Evans (1851–1941) excavated Cnossus in Crete, and these early archaeological endeavours provided the foundations for new knowledge about ancient Greece in the period preceding the earliest literary records. This new knowledge has tended to suggest that the culture and events of the Homeric poems have some basis in historical truth.

The island of Crete is the earliest centre of civilisation in the Mediterranean. The remains at Cnossus show that the Bronze Age civilisation called Minoan (from Minos, the mythical lawgiver of Crete) was highly developed and lasted from roughly 3000 to 1000BC. In mainland Greece, a Bronze Age civilisation, centred upon royal palaces such as those excavated at Mycenae, Tiryns and Pylos, developed somewhat later and lasted from 1580 to 1120BC. This civilisation is called Mycenaean, after what seems to have been its most powerful centre, Mycenae. In Homer, Agamemnon, leader of the

Greek expedition to Troy and the most powerful of the Greek princes, comes from Mycenae which Homer calls 'rich in gold', 'broad-streeted' and 'well-built'. In the Catalogue of Ships in Book II of the *Iliad* the largest numbers come from Mycenae and Pylos.

A script known as Linear B on clay tablets found at Pylos, Mycenae and Cnossus establishes strong links between Minoan and Mycenaean civilisations, and the decipherment of the script in the 1950s established that their common language was an archaic form of Greek. The extant tablets record accounts and inventories that have to do with the routine administration of the royal palaces. How widely the script was known and used cannot be ascertained. There is no evidence that it was used to record literature. The script is, comparatively speaking, a cumbersome one and could hardly have been used for a literary work of the length of the *Iliad*, even supposing that suitable materials such as leather or parchment were available. Nevertheless the existence of the script is an indication of the developed material culture of Mycenaean Greece.

After the destruction of Cnossus in 1400BC, Mycenaean civilisation was at its most powerful and advanced. The most substantial remains at Mycenae, the so-called Treasury of Atreus and the Tomb of Clytemnestra (Atreus was the father of Agamemnon and Clytemnestra was his wife) were built after 1300BC and the Lion Gate of Mycenae (so called from the relief over its lintel) dates from 1250BC. The fortification walls were mighty indeed. They were between twelve to forty-five feet thick and it has been estimated that they were as high as forty feet. The treasures found by Schliemann in the royal graves at Mycenae which include the famous gold face masks, bear witness to the opulent beauty of Mycenaean art work which was highly sophisticated in its craftsmanship and design. The techniques of engraving, enchasing and embossing were well developed and so was the art of inlaying bronze with precious metals. Ivory and amber imported from the east and the north are commonly found and indicate the extent of Mycenaean commercial relations. Mycenaean pottery of this period is found widely throughout the Mediterranean, a further indication that the Mycenaeans were great sailors and traders.

Excavations at Hissarlik, the site of Troy, have revealed nine settlements, the sixth settlement having substantial fortifications and monumental walls. The seventh of these settlements was destroyed in a great fire in the mid-thirteenth century BC, so that archaeological evidence seems to support the possibility of an historical Trojan War of which the Homeric account records the poetic memory. Soon after this possible date for the fall of Troy, Mycenaean power began to decline until in about 1120BC Mycenae and Tiryns and with them the Mycenaean culture of the Bronze Age were destroyed by the Dorians invading from the west. The Dorians were themselves Greek-speaking and possibly lived on the fringe of the Mycenaean empire. They initiated what is usually known as the Dark Ages, lasting from 1100 to 800BC. The Bronze Age gave way to the new Age of Iron. Refugees from the dispersal in mainland Greece created by the Dorian invasion now began to colonise the eastern seaboard of the Aegean Sea known as Ionia in Asia Minor. The Homeric poems are generally considered to have been composed in Ionia (largely on linguistic grounds); they may therefore preserve the memory of the Mycenaean mother culture transmitted by those who had colonised Asia Minor.

There are certainly relics of Mycenaean culture in the *Iliad*. It is generally agreed that the Catalogue of Ships in Book II is of early origin, and some scholars believe that it describes Greece as it was known in Mycenaean times. A more specific instance of a Mycenaean survival is the boar's tusk helmet of Odysseus described at X, 261–5. It is of a kind that is found in Mycenaean tombs and is not to be found in later excavations. The long body shield of Ajax worn without body armour (VII, 219–32) is Mycenaean and was gradually replaced by the smaller round shield with which a protective breastplate was worn. Homer mentions both kinds of armour. The historical mixture in the Homeric poems is well suggested by the use in them of both bronze and iron. Bronze is the principal metal used for armour and tools, but the heads of Pandarus's arrows are iron (IV, 123). Familiarity with iron is apparent in the use of it as a metaphor. When King Priam proposes to visit Achilles, his wife Hecabe exclaims that he must have a heart of iron (XXIV, 205) to visit the camp of the man who has killed so many of their sons. When Priam actually arrives, Achilles repeats the exclamation (XXIV, 521). The Homeric poems also record practices and customs that differ from those of Mycenaean times. For example, the Mycenaeans buried their dead, while in Homer the dead are cremated. In Mycenaean warfare one spear was used while Homer's warriors habitually carry two. Experts on warfare note that the tactics employed at XIII, 131–5 imply the use of the phalanx, an organised line of hoplites (infantrymen) that did not come into being until the development of the city state, possibly suggesting a date as late as 800BC. Some have thought that the scenes from ordinary life in the similes are those of Homer's own day and that Homer is deliberately drawing parallels between a heroic past and a humble present.

The language of Homer

Historians of the Greek language have identified the same kind of layered structure as that revealed by the archaeologists in which archaic elements co-exist side by side with later Ionic forms.. The language of Homer is a fusion of elements from various dialects the chief of which are the Ionic, the Aeolic, and the Arcadian. The predominant element is the Ionic, and this is the main reason for believing that the Homeric poems emanate from Ionia, but the Arcadian and Aeolic forms and vocabulary suggest that the Homeric epic has its roots in earlier times. The Arcadian and Aeolic dialects developed from dialects of Greek spoken in mainland Greece in the south and north respectively during the Mycenaean period. The fusion of these dialects with the Ionic has contributed to the view that Ionic bards took over and adapted to new circumstances and a new audience material which they had inherited from the past.

It is not simply the fusion of different dialect forms and vocabulary which suggests that the language of the Homeric poems has a long and complicated history. Study of Homeric composition has revealed a highly sophisticated process at work which can only have been refined over a long period of time. The process involves the development and use of formulae, the stock in trade of the oral poet who composed without the aid of writing. Some recurring Homeric formulae have become world-famous like 'the wine-dark sea', 'rosy-fingered dawn' or 'winged words'. Formulae may be short phrases like the above or may extend to longer passages describing often repeated actions such as the arming for battle, the preparation of a meal or the ritual of sacrifice. Formulae are convenient units that can be readily committed to memory and are therefore an aid to improvisation for the oral poet who is wholly dependent upon memory. In a famous study of Homeric formulae in the 1920s the American Homeric scholar Milman Parry (1902–35) demonstrated both the scope and economy of the system of formulaic composition.

It is necessary to have some rudimentary knowledge of Greek metre and the structure of the Greek language to understand how the formulaic system works. Homer's metre is the hexameter, a metre of six units (called feet); it is an arrangement of long and short syllables according to fixed rules. A long syllable followed by two short ones is called a dactyl (hence Homer's metre is often known as the dactylic hexameter) and two long syllables together are called a spondee. The scansion is as follows:

$$- \cup\cup \mid - \cup\cup \mid - \cup\cup \mid - \cup\cup \mid - \cup\cup \mid - - $$
$$- - \mid - - \mid - - \mid - - \mid \qquad\quad \mid - \cup$$

The first four feet may be either dactyls or spondees (with usually more dactyls than spondees). The fifth must be a dactyl and the final foot is never a dactyl but the second syllable may be short, thus making a trochee. Greek metre is quantitative, that is, words are fitted into the metrical pattern according to length of syllable. (In English metre the pattern is determined by accent, by the stress given to words in pronunciation.) Greek is an inflected language so that the forms of nouns and adjectives change according to the particular case in question, whether nominative, vocative, accusative, genitive, or dative.

Homer uses a number of adjectives to describe the hero of the *Iliad*, Achilles. All of these adjectives are generally appropriate to his character and role. But what Parry demonstrated is that in any particular context what governs the choice of a particular adjective is above all a metrical consideration. In the nominative case when he is the subject of a sentence Achilles is illustrious or swift-footed. He is only ever swift-footed in the nominative case. In the vocative, when anyone is addressing him, he is godlike. In the accusative when he is the object of a sentence he is illustrious. In the genitive case when he is possessing something he is always the son of Peleus. In the dative case when anyone is giving anything to him he is the shepherd of his people or a sacker of cities. The various noun/adjective combinations (sometimes there can be more than one adjective, for he can be both swift and illustrious together in the nominative case) all make different metrical patterns so that they can be slotted into the metre in different places. It has been calculated that there are fifty-six combinations of noun and adjective for Achilles. Each of these is determined by the case of the noun and by the position that the noun has in the verse, but no one of these combinations duplicates another; they are all metrically different. The scope is evident in the large number of combinations, over fifty, which have been developed to meet any syntactical and metrical need. The economy is evident in the fact that each of these combinations is unique, metrically speaking, and therefore allows the poet great flexibility in expression. Metre in any poetry determines what can and what cannot be said. What is remarkable about Parry's analysis of Homeric composition is that it suggests the restrictions inherent in oral composition and the extraordinary technical virtuosity through which they have been overcome.

The formulaic character of the Homeric epic can explain how it is that there are various layers, the earliest of which transmit relics of Mycenaean times. The oldest linguistic elements are probably what have come to be known as the 'traditional epithets', such as 'ox-eyed Hera', 'cloud-gathering Zeus' or 'Alalkomenaean Athene' some of which perplexed the Greeks themselves. The first systematic study of Homer in the late sixth century seems to have been concerned with the need to explain obsolete and difficult words. The formulaic character also explains why Homer's adjectives occasionally seem inappropriate in their particular context, why, for example, the sky is starry in the middle of the day (VIII, 46). Finally, the formulaic character of the epic goes some way to explain the obvious fact of repetition. About one third of the lines in the *Iliad* are repeated wholly or in part in the course of the poem. Equally one third is made up of phrases not found elsewhere. It is clear that the traditional inheritance was constantly being added to and varied to meet contemporary needs and the requirements of different tales. Homer's language therefore had been purposely developed for poetic recitation; it was never a spoken language. Nor did such a development, any more than the myths or the tales themselves, originate with one genius. There is a consensus of scholarly opinion that the language of *Iliad* and *Odyssey* evolved over many centuries and that its technique of formulaic diction goes back to the Mycenaean age from which it was no doubt transmitted by practising bards like Demodocus and Phemius in the *Odyssey*.

Some problems

But here the consensus stops and the Homeric question remains. The poetic excellence of the Homeric poems presupposes individual talent. Nobody can believe that countless other poems of the quality of the *Iliad* and *Odyssey* have been lost to us. Where does the individual talent stand in relation to the tradition? Most would say that 'Homer' came at the end of it. But was he a fully oral poet like Demodocus and Phemius, or did he use the oral method simply because he was composing for recitation? Did he dictate the text to a scribe, or did he write it himself? These are all open questions.

Comparisons with oral epics in other cultures show that in pre-literate cultures feats of memory that would be considered to be astonishing in a literate culture are common enough. Bards have recited from memory, or have improvised poems that are longer than the *Iliad*. But such poems are comparatively crude and do not have either the complex structure or the finished artistry of the Homeric poems. The difference in quality between the Homeric poems and oral epics in other cultures is more significant than anything that they have in common.

The problem is not made any easier by the inconclusive results of attempts to provide a date for the poems. The various layers that are apparent in the *Iliad* have been so fused that neither linguists nor archaeologists have been able to unravel the puzzle. Book X of the *Iliad* on various, chiefly linguistic grounds has been thought to be 'late', even by the ancient Greeks themselves. Yet ironically it contains what archaeologists recognise as one of the most obvious Mycenaean relics in the boar's tusk helmet worn by Odysseus. Nor have archaeologists been able to identify and provide a date for the most recent physical object in the poem. Most authorities envisage a date somewhere in the eighth century BC for the composition of the poems.

Nor is it known for certain when writing was introduced to Greece. Evidence suggests that knowledge and use of the syllabic Linear B script referred to earlier did not survive the fall of Mycenaean civilisation in the late twelfth century BC. Sometime between the tenth century and the eighth a new alphabetic script from Phoenicia was adopted in Greece. Papyrus (a form of paper originating in Egypt) seems not to have been introduced until later. Leather is known to have been used for writing quite early, though it would have been a costly business to commit a poem the size of the *Iliad* to leather. Any kind of book remained a rarity until the fifth century. Nevertheless the materials were available and it is theoretically possible that the poems were committed to writing at an early stage.

A note on the history of the written text

The earliest written text of Homer for which there is any evidence in Greek sources dates from the late sixth century BC when the Athenian leader of the day is reported to have brought texts of the poems to Athens and to have required the rhapsodes who recited Homer's poetry at the annual Athenian festival to do so one after another in proper order so that the poems would be recited as a whole. Given the special status of Homer in Greek culture from the earliest times, attested in the formation of special guilds of rhapsodes to recite the poems, it is certainly credible that there was a need for a definitive text.

The first textual criticism of Homer was carried out in the third and second centuries BC at Alexandria in the famous library there by a succession of scholars, the most notable of whom was Aristarchus (c.215–145BC). Many texts of Homer had been collected for the Alexandrian library and divergencies in the number of lines and variations in wording were glaringly apparent. At this time the Homeric text was standardised, and each poem was split up into twenty-four books, each given a letter of the Greek alphabet and a title heading still used to this day. This text standardised at Alexandria is the ancestor of all the texts that have come down to the modern world.

The Alexandrian version was copied like other ancient texts on papyrus rolls until the late second century AD when the codex (a book with pages) was introduced and papyrus was gradually replaced by the more durable parchment. The oldest surviving complete manuscripts are medieval, but fragments of the poems on papyrus survive from Graeco-Roman times. Some manuscripts preserve the opinions of the ancient commentators and the notes of Alexandrian textual critics in the form of scholia, comments written in the margins above and beside the text. Similar material is also incorporated in compilations made by Byzantine scholars from collections of material now lost. The most notable of these compilations is the vast commentary on the poems made sometime in the twelfth century by Eustathius, Archbishop of Thessalonika. These Byzantine commentaries, the scholia and ancient papyri have all been used by modern textual critics to arrive at the best possible text of the Homeric poems.

There have been many editions of the *Iliad* since the first edition printed in Florence in 1488. A reliable modern text of the Greek is the Oxford Classical Text of the *Iliad*, edited by T. W. Allen in three volumes, published by the Clarendon Press, Oxford, in 1931.

Part 2

Summaries
of THE ILIAD

THE NOTES THAT FOLLOW the summaries are designed to elucidate mythical and geographical references and to explain Greek antiquities. They deal with matters of substance rather than expression and can therefore be used with any reasonably close translation. The words in heavy type are either a literal version of what is in Homer, for example 'the will of Zeus' at the opening of the first book, or a summary version such as 'the laughter of the gods' for 'a fit of unquenchable laughter seized the gods' at the end of Book I. Occasionally the words in heavy type summarise whole incidents such as 'the sacrifice' (I, 458–63) about which a general point is being made. Most of the words explained or commented upon are proper names. The names are given in the form which is most often used in English, for example, Achilles, rather than Akilleus, Ajax rather than Aias. Most of the place names mentioned can be found on the map provided (p. 16).

Some cross-references are given to elucidate the structure of the poem or to suggest a recurring theme. These references are to the Greek and can therefore be looked up in any numbered modern text. The bilingual Loeb edition has the numbered Greek text with a translation on the facing page. Most translations also give Homer's line numbers. In the Penguin translation they are to be found at the top of each page.

A general summary

The poet calls upon the Muse to sing of the fatal anger of Achilles that brought countless woes to the Greeks and sent many noble souls of heroes to Hades before their time, in fulfilment of the will of Zeus after the quarrel broke out between Agamemnon, leader of the Greeks, and Achilles, their greatest fighter.

It is the ninth year of the siege of Troy. The god Apollo is angry because Agamemnon will not restore for ransom the daughter of one of his priests captured before the siege of Troy whom the Greek leader had taken as his prize in the general allotment of spoils. Apollo has sent a plague to infest the Greek camp. In a council called by Achilles to determine a course of action, Agamemnon quarrels with Achilles. He agrees to give up his prize but takes steps to make up his loss by

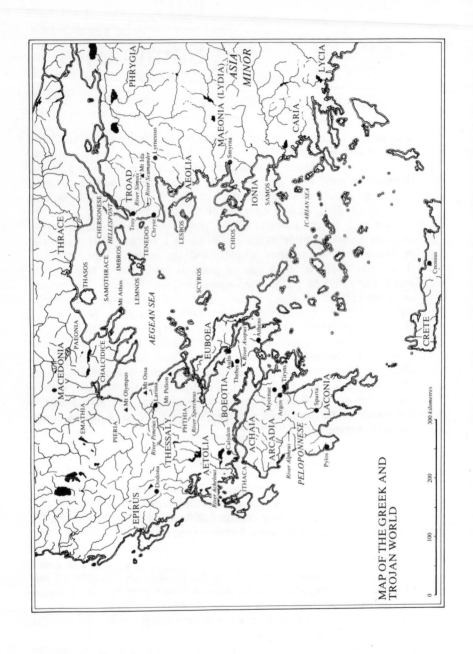

MAP OF THE GREEK AND
TROJAN WORLD

depriving Achilles of his spoil of war, Briseis. Thus slighted, Achilles withdraws from the fighting. He asks his goddess mother Thetis to persuade Zeus to grant the Trojans success so that the Greeks will be forced to recognise his worth. In a council upon Olympus, Zeus agrees to Thetis's request (Book I).

In the night Zeus sends a false dream of encouragement to Agamemnon who then tests the army. After a council the forces on both sides are marshalled and described (Book II). Paris and Menelaus fight a duel (Book III). The truce agreed for this duel is broken by Pandarus. Agamemnon inspects his troops (Book IV). Diomedes distinguishes himself in the fighting (Book V). Hector returns to the city to arrange for the Trojan women to propitiate Athene who has been helping Diomedes. He then returns to the battlefield, having said farewell to Andromache (Book VI). Hector and Ajax fight a duel which is interrupted by nightfall. In the evening a truce is made and a day is taken for the burial of the dead. In the following evening and night the Greeks build a wall to protect their ships (Book VII).

The next day sees the purposeful intervention of Zeus. The Trojans advance and encamp on the plain (Book VIII). Faced with this threat, the Greeks that same evening unsuccessfully petition Achilles (Book IX). During the night Odysseus and Diomedes reconnoitre the Trojan camp (Book X). The next day in spite of Agamemnon's early success Zeus promises Hector victory until sunset. The leading Greeks are wounded (Book XI), and the Trojans break through the wall (Book XII). Zeus takes his eye off the fighting, and Poseidon encourages the Greeks. Idomeneus distinguishes himself (Book XIII). Zeus is then lulled to sleep by Hera and the Greeks are able to forestall Trojan success again. Hector is wounded (Book XIV). Zeus awakes and fortunes are again reversed. The Trojans led by Hector break through to the ships (Book XV). Achilles allows Patroclus to fight in his armour to save the ships. Patroclus kills Sarpedon, and is then killed by Hector (Book XVI). In the struggle over the body of Patroclus, Menelaus distinguishes himself (Book XVII). News of Patroclus's death reaches Achilles. He grieves with Thetis, who promises him new armour. At sunset Hector rejects the advice of Polydamus to withdraw to the city. During the night Hephaestus makes Achilles's armour, while the Greeks mourn Patroclus (Book XVIII).

Next morning Achilles is presented with his new armour. In an assembly he renounces his anger. Agamemnon apologises and Briseis is restored. Preparations are made for battle (Book XIX). The fighting begins with Achilles dominant and the gods active on both sides (Book XX). Achilles presses the Trojans back to the river and fights with Scamander (Book XXI). Before the walls of Troy Hector is killed and mourned by the Trojans (Book XXII). In the evening there is a council and a meal in the Greek camp. That night the ghost of Patroclus appears to Achilles requesting burial. Next day Patroclus is buried and funeral games are held in his honour (Book XXIII). Achilles is sleepless. For the next eleven days at dawn he abuses Hector's corpse. On the twelfth Zeus orders him to desist. That night Priam visits his tent with a ransom for Hector. Achilles allows a truce for burial. The Trojans collect wood for nine days and on the next day Hector is buried (Book XXIV).

Detailed summaries

Book I   (The Plague. The Anger)

See the first two paragraphs of the general summary for a summary of this book.

NOTES AND GLOSSARY:

the Muse:
the goddess invoked by the poet is the muse. At I, 603 Homer refers to the muses singing on Mount Olympus, where the gods dwell. According to later writers there were nine muses who were the daughters of Zeus and Memory, each presiding over one of the major arts

Hades:
the underworld where the spirits of the dead dwell

Achaeans:
the Greeks; later Achaia was simply a part of Greece, in the northern Peloponnese

the will of Zeus:
Zeus is the son of Cronus, whose rule he overthrew, and parent of many of the other gods. He is the most powerful of the Olympians, often referred to as their king, and his special province is the upper air where he controls storms and clouds, and sends rain. His power is expressed in his thunderbolt. Another of his emblems is the eagle. At I, 523 Zeus accedes to the request of Thetis, the mother of Achilles, that her son be avenged for the dishonour done to him by Agamemnon

Agamemnon:
the leader of the Greek expedition against Troy

Achilles, son of Peleus: the use of a patronymic is a common way of describing a character in Homer

chaplet:
a fillet made of wool; when wound around a staff it was a sign of the suppliant or one who was a priest. Suppliants and priests were protected by the gods

the sons of Atreus: Agamemnon and Menelaus

Olympus:	a high mountain on the Greek mainland where it was believed the gods dwelt
Argos:	Greece generally, not merely the town of Argos
Chryse, Cilla, Tenedos:	all places near Troy. Tenedos is an island
Smintheus:	only occurs here, meaning possibly killer of mice
Danaans:	the Greeks (also called Achaeans or Argives)
Phoebus:	means 'shining', an appropriate epithet of the sun god; his sister Artemis, the moon goddess, is also called Phoebe
white-armed Hera:	the epithet probably suggests beauty. Hera is the wife and sister of Zeus. She is a powerful goddess who supports the Greek cause as a result of the judgment of Paris (see XXIV, 25–30). Zeus gave Paris, the second son of King Priam of Troy, the task of deciding which of the three senior goddesses, Hera, Athene and Aphrodite, was the fairest. Hera offered Paris wealth and power, Athene offered him renown in war and Venus offered him the most beautiful woman in the world, Helen, wife of the Greek Menelaus. Paris chose Aphrodite and her gift. This judgment not only offended Hera and Athene but caused the Trojan War. The Greeks sent an expedition to recover Helen after Paris had abducted her to Troy
an augur:	one who tells the future (usually by observing the behaviour of birds), a prophet
another prize:	when the Greeks sacked cities it was customary to divide the spoils of war, women, horses, armour, among the victors according to status and merit. As these prizes were a mark of honour, it is natural that Agamemnon should demand a replacement. The link between prizes and honour is crucial to the outbreak of the quarrel
captured towns:	compare line 366 and also VI, 415 and IX, 328–9
Phthia:	Achilles's homeland in Thessaly in northern Greece
Myrmidons:	the Thessalian people of whom Achilles was chief. The word is derived from the Greek word for ant. Zeus had created men from ants for Achilles's grandfather Aeacus, who was alone without a people
Athene:	the virgin warrior goddess who sprang from the head of Zeus. Her flashing eyes denote spirit and power

aegis-bearing Zeus: the aegis (literally, a storm cloud) is a heavy shield with a hundred gold tassels, the means of raising tempests and creating panic among mortals (see V, 738)

Atreides: *ides* means 'son of'. The son of Atreus, Agamemnon

Hector: the chief warrior among the Trojans, as Achilles is the chief warrior among the Greeks

Nestor: a wise old man, if somewhat garrulous. He is king of Pylos in the eastern Peloponnese

Pirithous and Dryas: these older heroes took part in the battle between the Lapiths and the centaurs, the latter a race of creatures half man half horse. Nestor makes the distinction between the two leaders clear. Agamemnon has greater prestige because he rules over more people; Achilles is the stronger and owes his strength to his goddess mother Thetis, a sea nymph daughter of Nereus

Briareus: his father was Uranus, Sky

Son of Cronos: Zeus, who deposed his father. Relations between the gods were not often harmonious. There is no other reference to this story in Homer or elsewhere

Achilles's short life: his mother told him that he was fated either to gain glory and die early or to live a long but inglorious life. Achilles chose glory and knew that he would not return from the Trojan War (see IX, 410-16). Given this choice, any loss of honour was especially difficult to bear

Ocean: in Homer it was thought to encircle the earth

Ethiopians: from the Homeric point of view they were a remote people living at the edge of the world

the sacrifice: the thighs wrapped in fat and soaked in wine were offered to the gods

Thetis clasps Zeus's knees: the usual mode of supplication

the ambrosial hair of Zeus: ambrosial means 'immortal'. Ambrosia is the food of the gods, nectar their drink

Hephaestus: the god of fire and of metalwork. He makes the armour of Achilles in Book XVIII

Lemnos: an island in the Aegean Sea

the laughter of the gods: a famous comic moment

Book II (The Dream. The Catalogue of Ships)

Zeus sends a false dream to Agamemnon to tell him that he can now take Troy. Agamemnon decides to test his troops by telling them that he has been told by Zeus that his cause is lost. The soldiers rush to the ships and have to be rallied by Odysseus. There follows a council in which Thersites, a common soldier, rails against Agamemnon, and is beaten by Odysseus who restores good morale. Nestor advises Agamemnon to marshal his troops and there follows a long catalogue of the forces of the Greeks, and of the Trojans they face.

NOTES AND GLOSSARY:

the False Dream: Homer has been much criticised for allowing Zeus to engage in such a wilful deception

a tunic: a close-fitting shift made of linen which reached below the knees. A large woollen cloak thrown over the shoulders was worn out of doors

the council: this is the clearest picture in the poem of prevailing Greek institutions consisting of three parts: the king, the council of elders and the assembly of the whole people

Agamemnon's test: it is difficult to say why Agamemnon should have decided to do this

the staff: the description of its ancestry adds to the dignity of its possessor and confirms the close relation between gods and kings. Hermes is the messenger of the gods. He guides Priam to the tent of Achilles in the final book. Argus was a monster with a hundred eyes whom the suspicious Hera had ordered to watch Io, a maiden beloved by Zeus whom Zeus had turned into a cow to avoid detection by Hera. Pelops won his wife Hippodamia in a chariot race. Thyestes is the brother of Atreus, father of Agamemnon

Agamemnon's speech: indirectly sets the wider context of the present action of the poem with its mention that the siege has already lasted nine years

Icarian Sea: south-eastern part of the Aegean sea

Athene and Odysseus: Athene, the goddess of wisdom, naturally seeks out the most quick-witted of the Greeks

Ithaca: an island on the western coast of Greece which was the home of Odysseus

Thersites: the only commoner to play a part in the poem. His physical deformity accords well with his abusive behaviour. He taunts Agamemnon in a manner similar to that of Achilles in Book I, and calls to mind the quarrel between the two leading Greeks. A famous episode

Telemachus: the young son whom Odysseus left behind when he went to Troy. He figures prominently in the *Odyssey*, especially in Books I–IV

Aulis: a coastal town in Boeotia in northern Greece. Here in later accounts (though not in Homer) Agamemnon was forced to sacrifice his daughter Iphigeneia to the goddess Artemis in order to gain a favourable wind to sail for Troy

Scamander: the river that has its source on Mount Ida and flows through the plain of Troy, sometimes called Xanthos, 'the yellow river'

the Catalogue: the similes which introduce it are justly famous. The catalogue itself has been much discussed by commentators ancient and modern. In some manuscripts it is found with a separate heading; in others it is omitted altogether. Scholars agree that it is genuine and is of early origin, transmitting information from Mycenaean times. Whether it is a poetic fiction or a true historical record has been much debated. It has the effect of widening the scope of the poem to include much of the then known Greek world. Homer starts with the Boeotians in central Greece and moves south to the Peloponnese, then to the western islands, whence to Crete and the southern islands of the Aegean and back to the mainland. The total number of ships is more than one thousand

Ares: the god of war

Thamyris: a mythological excursus is inserted into the list as a diverting aside. A challenge to the gods brings its inevitable penalty

Heracles: the most famous Greek hero of an earlier generation

Lyrnessus: it is near Thebe, already mentioned by Achilles (I, 366)

Philoctetes: later writers tell how Troy could only be taken with his bow and arrows, which had been a present from Heracles

Styx: a river in Hades (meaning 'hate') by which the gods swear inviolable oaths

Telamonian Ajax:	there are two Greeks called Ajax in Homer. The other is the son of Oileus
Iris:	a messenger of the gods who often takes the form of a rainbow. Here she takes the form of a mortal

---

Book III (The Truce. The View from the Walls. The Duel of Paris and Menelaus)

The two armies meet on the Trojan plain. Paris challenges the Greeks to single combat. Menelaus takes up the challenge, and Paris momentarily retires daunted. Hector upbraids Paris who then proposes a truce and a formal duel between himself and Menelaus to settle the issue of the war between them. Hector sends messengers to summon Priam. From the walls of Troy, Helen shows Priam the Greek leaders. A truce is made and oaths are taken. In the duel Menelaus defeats Paris who is rescued by Aphrodite and returned to Troy. Aphrodite summons Helen to Paris. Recriminations follow. Agamemnon proclaims Menelaus victor.

NOTES AND GLOSSARY:

Pigmies:	the battle of the cranes and the pigmies (a people of small size) supposedly took place annually with the winter migration of the cranes to the warmer climate of Africa, in the Homeric world view a land at the edge of the earth
the truce:	the challenge and the duel are chivalrously conducted according to set formulae involving oath-taking, sacrifice and prayer. Both Greeks and Trojans observe the same code of battle, have the same religious ritual and arm themselves in the same way
the web:	weaving is a traditional activity for women in Homer. Andromache is weaving when she hears news of Hector's death
the Scaean Gate:	on the western side of Troy facing the sea. The famous scene that follows is often called the Teichoscopia, the view from the wall
cicada:	a grasshopper, a famous simile
Priam and Helen:	Priam blames the gods, not Helen. In reply Helen seems to accept responsibility for her part in the abduction
Antenor and Odysseus:	before the war, Odysseus had visited Troy with Menelaus to try to regain Helen by peaceful means (compare XI, 124 where it is said that Paris bribed the negotiators to reject Greek overtures)

Menelaus:	here characterised as being a man of few words. He came from Sparta in Laconia. The Spartans were famous for their taciturnity; whence the meaning of the word 'laconic'
Phrygia:	a region east of Troy. The Amazons were women warriors who cut off their right breasts in order to use the bow more efficiently. They lived near the Caucasus
Helen's brothers:	Helen does not know that they are already dead. Homer rarely intervenes in his own narrative and when he does so, it is usually as here for ironic or pathetic effect
the prayer to Zeus:	in spite of this there is little indication that the gods punished mortals in life or after death for breaking oaths. In the Homeric after-life what survives is only the faintest shadow of a man, incapable of feeling joy or pain
greaves:	pieces of armour which protect the legs from the ankles to the knees
a cuirass:	a breastplate
Paris and Aphrodite:	the gods intervene in battle scenes as in every aspect of life in Homer. Paris is Aphrodite's favourite as a result of the Judgment of Paris explained above. She is the goddess of beauty as well as of love so that her devotee Paris is himself handsome, dresses well and is described in beautiful surroundings (notice his perfumed bedroom)
Helen and Aphrodite:	the disguise of the goddess is to conceal her from others. Helen's initial refusal to obey her creates sympathy for her and underlines Aphrodite's power. The love goddess is not only seductive but threatening
Maeonia:	like Phrygia it lies east of Troy, even further from Helen's native Greece

---

Book IV (The Breaking of the Truce. Agamemnon marshals his Troops)

In a council upon Olympus, to annoy Hera Zeus proposes that the terms of the truce be honoured and the war ended with Menelaus's victory. Hera opposes this. The gods agree to arrange for the truce to be broken. Athene in disguise persuades Pandarus to shoot Menelaus with an arrow. He is wounded. Agamemnon marshals his troops and the armies engage.

NOTES AND GLOSSARY:

Hebe: daughter of Zeus and Hera. Her name denotes youthful beauty. She is cupbearer to the gods

Alalkomenean: the meaning of the word is not known

when it is my turn: this kind of argument shows the gods in a very poor light, squabbling like children with little regard to anything other than their own whims and pleasures. Zeus here shows no hostility to the Trojans. On the contrary he approves of their piety. Nor does he show any sign of taking the serious view of their perjury held by the Greeks

Pandarus: comes from Lycia, a region south-east of Troy famous for its archers and for the shrine of Apollo at Patara

the bow: the arrowhead is of iron. Most weapons in Homer are made of bronze

the corselet: made of two curved plates of bronze, one for the breast and one for the back, which overlapped at each side. They were kept in place with a clasp at the shoulder and with a belt at the waist. The arrow landed on the golden buckle of the belt where it lay over the two overlapping edges of the breast and back plates. Below the corselet was a girdle of metal plates lined with wool which further protected the waist and abdomen. The apron, made of leather, was beneath the girdle and covered the lower abdomen and upper thighs

Caria and Maeonia: regions far to the south and east of Troy

Agamemnon's prediction: it is echoed by Hector at VI, 448

Asclepius: a son of Apollo, god of healing

Cheiron: a centaur, half horse, half man, famous for his knowledge and wisdom. He taught the young Achilles and several other Greek heroes

Nestor's tactics: the experienced old soldier persistently gives advice to Agamemnon, first in the opening quarrel, when the army has regrouped after fleeing to the ships, and now here in the matter of strategy. In fact the fighting subsequently centres upon the exploits of individual heroes. There is no attempt to keep in line as Nestor suggests

Ereuthalion: see VII, 136

the insult to Odysseus: although Agamemnon withdraws it, this is further indication of his quick temper and bad judgment

Tydeus:	one of the seven heroes, the 'seven against Thebes', who tried to restore Polyneices, one of the sons of Oedipus, to Thebes after he had been expelled by his brother Eteocles who refused to share the kingship with him. The Asopus is a river south of Thebes
Capaneus:	another of the famous seven against Thebes which was eventually captured by the sons of the seven
boss:	the boss of a shield is the protuberance at its centre
spoil:	it is an essential part of the fight that the killer should despoil the victim of his armour, not so much for its value, as for the visible prestige involved
Simois:	the second river of Troy rising on Mount Ida and flowing into the Scamander
Pergamus:	the word means 'citadel', and is often used for the citadel of Troy where Apollo had a temple

Book V   (The Aristeia of Diomedes)

Diomedes distinguishes himself. Inspired by Athene, he drives the Trojans before him. He is wounded by an arrow from Pandarus, but is strengthened and encouraged by Athene who removes mist from his eyes so that he can recognise the gods. She permits him to fight against Aphrodite. Diomedes encounters Pandarus whom he kills and Aeneas whom he wounds with a stone. Aphrodite rescues Aeneas, and is then herself wounded by Diomedes. Apollo and Ares now help the Trojans. Hector, rebuked by Sarpedon, revives the Trojans and Diomedes retreats. Athene rebukes him and together they wound Ares.

NOTES AND GLOSSARY:

Diomedes:	this book contains his 'aristeia', that is deeds of bravery done by him
Artemis:	sister of Apollo and the goddess of chastity and hunting. As Apollo is the sun god, Artemis is the moon goddess
Meriones:	Athene is the goddess of the mechanical arts and so favours Meriones, a carpenter
the river god Scamander:	rivers in Homer are personified. Achilles fights Scamander in Book XXI
Athene's encouragement:	a mortal could not fight against an immortal without the support of another god
the horses of the breed of Tros:	a pair of divine horses descended from the north wind Boreas (whence they derived their speed) were given to Tros, an early king of Troy

which took its name from him, in return for his son Ganymede, a beautiful youth beloved by Zeus and taken up to Olympus by him to be the cupbearer of the gods

Anchises: the horses belonged to the successors of Tros. Anchises was the younger brother of Laomedon, father of Priam and king before him

Cyprian Aphrodite: Aphrodite is associated with Cyprus because she came to the island soon after her birth

Enyo: personification of the tumult of battle, a companion of Ares

the Graces: three sisters who gave festive joy and were associated with refinement and beauty, and so appropriate robe-makers to the goddess of beauty and love

Otus and Ephialtes: these giants piled Pelion on Ossa and Ossa on Olympus (all mountains) in order to storm heaven (see *Odyssey* XI, 308). They were killed by Apollo. The Olympians had come to power by force

Hera and Heracles: Heracles was a son of Zeus by Alcmene. His stepmother Hera hated him from birth; she sent two snakes to kill him in his cradle. Heracles strangled them

Hades: not only the kingdom of the dead but also the king himself. One of Heracles's labours was the task of fetching Cerberus, the three-headed dog, who guarded the entrance to the underworld

Paeeon: in Greek the name means 'he who heals'

Aegialea: Adrastus was one of the seven against Thebes. There is no other mention in Homer of the fate of Diomedes. In other writers he is one of the few Greeks to return home unscathed

Leto: the mother of Apollo and Artemis

Ares: particularly associated with Thrace, so that it is appropriate that he should take the form of a Thracian captain

Demeter: the goddess of agriculture; not often mentioned in Homer

Alpheus: a river in the Peloponnese

Pylaemenes: killed here, he is alive in Book XIII where he mourns the death of his son

Heracles: he saved Hesione, the daughter of Laomedon, king of Troy. He then attacked and captured Troy because the king failed to give him his promised

	reward, mares from the stock of the horses of Tros
Sarpedon:	a son of Zeus. His death in Book XVI is foreshadowed here
the Gorgon's head:	the sight of the Gorgon Medusa was so terrible that she turned to stone all who looked upon her. She was slain by Perseus with the help of a mirror provided by Athene
Stentor:	means in Greek 'roarer' from which the English 'stentorian'
Dardanian:	Trojan: Dardanus was one of the founders of the Trojan race
the sons of Uranus:	probably refers to the Titan whom the Olympian gods displaced

---

Book VI   (The Conversation of Hector and Andromache)

The continuing Greek success prompts Helenus to advise his brother Hector to persuade the Trojan women to propitiate Athene. On the battlefield Diomedes encounters Glaucus and on recognising that they are hereditary guest friends, they exchange armour and part in friendship. Meanwhile Hector delivers his message to Hecabe, and goes to the house of Paris to persuade him to fight. Helen also rebukes Paris. Hector then meets Andromache with their son on the tower and bids farewell to her before returning together with Paris to the fighting.

NOTES AND GLOSSARY:

the robe called a peplos:	on the frieze of the temple of the Parthenon on the Athenian Acropolis there is a depiction of the presentation of the peplos to Athene
Diomedes to Glaucus:	given that he has just wounded Aphrodite and Ares, it is strange that Diomedes says he will not fight against Glaucus if he proves to be a god. The inconsistency has been much debated
Dionysus:	the god of wine and intoxication. He was brought up in a cave near Mount Nysa in Thrace
the generations of men like leaves:	these lines are among the most celebrated in Homer
Sisyphus:	his wickedness in life was punished in the underworld where he had to roll up hill a huge stone which rolled back every time it reached the top
the tablet:	the only reference in Homer to anything that could be a kind of writing
the Chimaera:	the only example in Homer of a hybrid monster.

Bellerophon's exploits represent a different kind of heroism from that celebrated in the *Iliad*. His tasks are like the labours of Heracles. Homer does not mention the winged horse Pegasus with which Bellerophon is associated in later writers

always excel: a famous line repeated at XI, 784 where it is advice given by Peleus to Achilles

the exchange of gold for bronze: this line became proverbial. The two heroes chivalrously feel the inherited obligations of guest friendship. An exchange of gifts was customary. Compare also the exchange of gifts between Hector and Ajax at VII, 290–2

Sidon: in Phoenicia, a region of developed culture. The Phoenicians were great traders

Acropolis: the high point of the city

eleven cubits: a sixteen-foot spear

Eetion: referred to at I, 364

Astyanax: the name means 'leader of the city'. The name Hector means 'defender'

the burial of Eetion: here Achilles follows the usual heroic code in allowing burial to an enemy. The contrast with his treatment of Hector is foreshadowed

oracles: according to some accounts when Poseidon and Apollo built the walls of Troy, a mortal helped them at one point; here only the walls might be breached

Hector's prophecy: echoes Agamemnon's at IV, 163–5. Compare his earlier foreboding at lines 366–7

the loom and the spindle: in Homeric society the sexes have very distinct roles

the stallion: the simile is repeated with reference to Hector at XV, 263–8

Book VII   (The Duel between Hector and Ajax. Burial of the Dead)

Hector issues a challenge to single combat. The Greeks draw lots and Ajax confronts Hector. In the fight Ajax gets the better of Hector. Heralds from both sides intervene; the heroes stop fighting and exchange gifts. That evening Nestor proposes a truce for the burial of the dead. In Troy Antenor advises the return of Helen and her property. Paris will not let Helen go, but is prepared to surrender her goods. The Greeks reject the Trojan offer but agree to a truce for the burial of the dead. They also decide to dig a trench and build a high wall to protect their ships.

NOTES AND GLOSSARY:

Hector's conditions: the proper burial rites were necessary to enable the souls of the departed to enter Hades

Hellespont: the narrow strait between the Trojan plain and the Thracian Chersonese, now dividing Europe from Asia

Peleus: see XI, 765 where Nestor's visit to Peleus to recruit Achilles is referred to

Ereuthalion: mentioned earlier by Nestor at IV, 319. It is part of his character that he looks back to past exploits which he relates somewhat garrulously

Mount Ida: it rises to the east of Troy

silent prayers: the idea is to prevent the enemy using the same formula to counter-persuade the god in question. Characteristically Ajax puts belief in his own powers before any such superstition

Hyle: in Boeotia

the first shot: usually decided by lot, so that Hector feels affronted that Ajax should give him an apparent advantage, thus asserting his own superiority

the exchange of gifts: such magnanimity is characteristic of Hector, the most chivalrous of the heroes at Troy

Nestor's advice: there are two strange features of this speech. The custom of taking bones home (difficult from a communal burning) is not referred to elsewhere in Homer. As the Greeks are winning, it is not obvious why the proposal to build a defensive wall should be made here

Paris: the Trojans despise Paris and even the herald Idaeus boldly curses him, yet Paris is allowed a veto in matters that concern him

Poseidon: the god of the sea, but also the god who can make the earth quake. He was cheated by Laomedon of his payment for building the walls of Troy. He opposes the Trojan cause

Jason: an earlier hero, the leader of the Argonauts who had sailed after the golden fleece

---

Book VIII   (The Interrupted Fight)

Zeus calls a council and forbids the gods to intervene on either side, saying that he is determined to bring the war to a close. From Mount Ida he encourages the Trojans, sending thunderbolts among the Greeks and causing them to flee before Hector. Hera and Athene, who realise that Zeus is honouring his promise to Thetis, prepare to help the Greeks but are driven back in fright by Zeus's anger. Night falls, and the Trojans encamp on the battlefield in front of the newly built wall.

NOTES AND GLOSSARY:

Tartarus: a place of punishment for rebellious gods; see lines 479–81

the golden chain: a much allegorised passage

Gargaron: the summit of Mount Ida

the scales of Zeus: a dramatic figurative expression for the workings of fate. Whether the notion implies a fate which is beyond the will of Zeus (rather than merely being its expression) has been much debated

Zeus thunders: the Trojan victory is brought about directly by the intervention of Zeus in fulfilment of his promise to Thetis given in Book I. See also lines 133 and 170

drink and the feast: as a sign of honour (compare VII, 321)

Helice and Aegae: both on the northern coast of the Peloponnese; notable shrines to Poseidon

eagle: the bird of Zeus

Teucer the bastard child: when Heracles sacked Troy he took away Hesione and gave her as a slave to Telamon. Teucer was their offspring, his name indicating his Trojan descent

a tripod: a three-legged kettle for warming water

with the eyes of a Gorgon: that is, with a look that inspires great terror

Eurystheus: a king of Mycenae for whom Heracles performed his twelve labours

Erebos: meaning 'darkness', another name for the underworld. Styx, the river of hate, is in Hades

Iapetos and Cronos: Titans, sons of Uranus overthrown by the Olympians

the Trojan fires: the night piece with which the book closes is much celebrated

---

Book IX (The Embassy to Achilles. Prayers)

The Greeks are in a state of panic. Agamemnon calls an assembly and suggests flight. Diomedes rebukes him, and Nestor suggests a private council in which he proposes that they immediately propitiate Achilles. Agamemnon agrees, offering princely gifts and the restoration of Briseis. Ajax, Odysseus, and Phoenix, Achilles's aged retainer, go by night to Achilles's tent to make the appeal. Achilles is not moved, and the ambassadors return to report failure.

NOTES AND GLOSSARY:

Agamemnon's speech: repeated from II, 110–18 and 139–41

Diomedes's reply: refers back to Agamemnon's speech at IV, 370–400

Nestor's speech: as usual he offers practical advice for the immediate present. In his second speech he defines the obligations of the king, and clearly blames Agamemnon for not having followed his advice in the initial quarrel. Agamemnon admits his folly

tripods: kettles untouched by the flames, that is, new

a bride for Achilles: the usual practice was for the bridegroom to give large sums to the father of the bride. Agamemnon offers to reverse the practice

seven towns: presumably tributary states. Agamemnon offers substantial gifts, but still requires that Achilles submit

Achilles sings of the deeds of heroes: illustrating clearly the connection between the hero, fame and song

the ship's heads: in which the sterns of the vessels terminated. They were probably ornamental and were probably used as trophies

Peleus: Odysseus and Nestor recruited Achilles from him for the war

Odysseus's speech: it repeats Agamemnon's offer verbatim, but omits Agamemnon's requirement that Achilles should submit. Odysseus skilfully saves his most persuasive appeal – to Achilles's desire for glory – until the end

Orchomenos and Egyptian Thebes: both legendary for their wealth; the only mention of Egypt in the poem

rocky Pytho: Apollo's famous oracle at Delphi was called Pytho after the dragon killed there by Apollo. Rich offerings were brought to the oracle by those consulting it

Achilles's choice: famous throughout antiquity, as was the choice of Heracles who chose virtue rather than pleasure. Achilles in anger here renounces the heroic impulse that motivated him at Troy

Hellas: not, as later, the whole of Greece, for which Homer's word is normally Achaia

the Furies: divinities that guarded parental rights, and closely associated with gods of the underworld

the Prayers: the only developed allegory in Homer. The prayers follow upon Ate which means 'folly' or 'infatuation' though it is often translated as 'sin', as penitence might follow upon wrongdoing. If the injured party listens to the prayers, he will be rewarded; if not he too will be visited by Ate

the story of Meleager: the longest exemplary myth in Homer. The poet typically starts in the middle and then goes back in time. Calydon is in the north-west of Greece

Alcyone: the Greek word for kingfisher

Ajax's speech: his blunt reply expresses the straightforwardness of his character. To him it seems a simple matter, for the social customs of the time allow for more serious offences (such as the killing of kin) to be paid for by compensation. In reply Achilles says he cannot stomach the way he has been treated like a newcomer, that is, one who has no kin to avenge him

Achilles's last words: they show that he really has no intention of leaving for home. He will fight when Hector reaches his ship

---

Book X   (The Dolon episode)

That same night, the Greek camp being in further confusion, Nestor suggests that spies be sent to discover Trojan intentions. Odysseus and Diomedes volunteer. They capture the Trojan spy Dolon who has been sent by Hector on a similar errand, and he tells them of the prize horses of the newly arrived Thracian king Rhesus who is encamped nearby. Diomedes kills Dolon: the sleeping Rhesus and his followers are killed and his horses are captured.

NOTES AND GLOSSARY:

Odysseus's helmet: such an helmet is known to have been worn in the Mycenaean period only, and not subsequently. The description must have come down from a period before the poem was composed

Autolycus: the grandfather of Odysseus

Tydeus at Thebes: see IV, 396 and V, 803

Ilus: king of Troy, grandfather of Priam. Troy (Ilium) was named after him

Dolon's death: the killing of an unarmed suppliant in such a manner has been thought beneath the dignity of an Homeric hero

tamarisk: a marsh shrub

polished baths and olive oil: the Greeks have with them the amenities of civilisation

Book XI   (The Aristeia of Agamemnon)

The Greeks led by Agamemnon push the Trojans back to the Scaean Gate. Hector is warned by Zeus to retreat until Agamemnon retires. Thereafter he is promised glory until sunset. Agamemnon is wounded. Hector returns and is checked by Diomedes who is then wounded by an arrow from Paris. Odysseus is wounded and retires. Hector advances, forcing the Greeks onto the defensive. Machaon, wounded by Paris, is taken back to the Greek camp by Nestor. Hector forces Ajax to retire. Achilles sees Nestor returning with Machaon and sends Patroclus to discover who the wounded man is. Nestor advises Patroclus to persuade Achilles to send him and the Myrmidons to their aid.

NOTES AND GLOSSARY:

Tithonus: brother of Priam, he was given immortality by Zeus at the Dawn's request. She forgot to ask for eternal youthfulness. This is the third day of fighting after Achilles's withdrawal

Cinyras: later famous as a king of Cyprus

Agamemnon's armour: a broad belt, stretching from the right or left shoulder diagonally across the body to suspend the sword

the Gorgon: the three-headed monster has snakes for hair so that the description of the twisting enamel is particularly apt and artful

Achilles accepted a ransom: in the present action of the poem, though many captives plead for their lives, no ransom is accepted on the battlefield

like a lion: Agamemnon, king of men, is compared four times to a lion, king of beasts. See lines 129, 173, 238

the Greek embassy: see III, 205

Zeus's message: Zeus promises Hector supremacy only until sunset. Hector forgets this limitation

the Eileithyiae: meaning the twisters, daughters of Hera, the goddess of childbirth

Diomedes insults Hector: his words are repeated by Achilles at XX, 449–54

Paris uses his bow: the contempt expressed by Diomedes for the bowman is felt throughout the poem where all the fighting is essentially hand-to-hand combat between armed warriors

Odysseus's indecision: the internal debate contrasts with the more physical reactions of Ajax when similarly outnumbered later at line 544

Ajax like a lion and like an ass: the juxtaposition of these two celebrated similes produces a striking effect. The lion simile is repeated at XVII, 657–66. The ass simile has been much criticised on the grounds that it is demeaning for a hero to be compared to such a lowly beast

Achilles takes note: Homer here advances the plot by making Achilles send Patroclus to Nestor who makes the fatal suggestion that leads to Patroclus's death (lines 796–803)

Nestor's cup: this closely resembles a golden cup discovered in the graves at Mycenae

Patroclus speaks about Achilles: even his friend finds him difficult. To the Greeks he is a thorn in their flesh as Paris is to the Trojans

Nestor's youthful exploits: as always Nestor looks to the past. He compares his unselfish valour with that of Achilles

Heracles: here apparently a destructive figure

Augeas: famous for the stables cleaned by Heracles as one of his labours

the Moliones: see XXIII, 638

Peleus's advice: that given to Glaucus at VI, 208

Cheiron: a centaur (half man, half horse) who educated Achilles

---

Book XII (The Battle for the Wall)

The Trojans led by Hector cross the trench on foot and attempt to break through the wall. Sarpedon leads the decisive attack with Glaucus and the Lycians. Mnestheus, Ajax and Teucer oppose them. Finally, Hector breaks the gate with a great stone, and leads the Trojans into the Greek camp.

NOTES AND GLOSSARY:

the wall: the failure to make proper offerings causes Apollo and Poseidon who had built the walls of Troy to destroy them

the trident: a spear with three prongs which is the emblem of Poseidon's power

Asius: his story is resumed at XIII, 384

the Lapithae: these people had fought a famous battle with the centaurs

Polydamas: he had offered advice that Hector had been pleased to take earlier (lines 60–80)

Hector rebukes Polydamas: this is one of the most celebrated speeches in the poem. Hector rejects superstitious fears and

omens, putting his faith in Zeus. It contains a
famous patriotic sentiment appropriate to Hector
on whose prowess his country depends

the speech of Sarpedon: another celebrated speech epitomising 'the
heroic code'

the two men quarrelling: the simile implies a system of agriculture
similar to the strip farming common in medieval
Europe with equitable distribution of land among
members of the community. The *Iliad* is notable
for the variety of its similes

Book XIII   (The Battle at the Ships)

Zeus turns his eyes from the battle. Poseidon comes to the aid of the
Greeks. Idomeneus does great deeds. Hector confronts Ajax. The
Trojan advance is checked.

NOTES AND GLOSSARY:

Mysians: these people came from the north, from southern
Russia and the lower Danube

Samothrace: an island north west of Troy in the Thracian Sea.
The plain of Troy can be seen from its high
mountains

Aegae: no such place near Troy has been identified by
commentators

Tenedos and Imbros: islands off the coast of Troy

joy of battle: the Greek word is *charma*. War is also regarded as
hateful. There are many attitudes to war in the
Iliad

Poseidon blames Agamemnon: this recapitulates the main theme

Imbrius: most of the Trojans whose deaths are dwelt upon
are in some way related to Priam and the royal
house

Poseidon and Zeus: they were both sons of Cronos and Rhea. Although
Zeus has more power and knowledge than other
Olympians, he is clearly neither omnipotent nor
omniscient, even though sometimes he is addressed
as such by other characters in the poem

Cassandra: this tragic figure is mentioned only twice in the
poem

Aeneas resents Priam: no explanation is given for this in the poem

a bronze axe: not used as a weapon elsewhere in Homer, nor is
the sling referred to here

Pylaemenes: already killed at V, 576

Book XIV   (The Deception of Zeus)

The Greek leaders, nursing their wounds in the Greek camp, respond to the sound of the fighting with a new resolve, encouraged by Poseidon. Hera borrows Aphrodite's girdle, obtains the help of Sleep and lulls Zeus to sleep on Mount Ida. Poseidon further encourages the Greeks. Hector is knocked unconscious by a stone thrown by Ajax. The Trojans are driven back from the wall.

NOTES AND GLOSSARY:

Odysseus rebukes Agamemnon: the latter is again shown in a poor light as a weak leader prone to depression

Tydeus: migrated to Argos because he had killed someone, according to later accounts. Diomedes passes over the incident in silence

Athene: as the goddess of the mechanical arts, she presides over spinning and weaving, and so makes a robe for Hera

Oceanus and Tethys: usually regarded as the children of Uranus (sky) and Earth. Here they seem to be primal beings

Rhea: wife of Cronos who was ousted by Zeus

Pieria: a region in Thessaly bordering on Olympus

Emathia: to the north of Pieria in Macedonia. Athos is a mountain on the Chalcidian peninsula. Lemnos is an island opposite Troy

Heracles: see V, 640; XV, 18–30; XIX, 96–133

the Graces: beautiful daughters of Zeus

Titans: pre-Olympian gods who had been banished to Tartarus by Zeus

Lecton: a southern spur of Mount Ida

Ixion's wife: Dia

daughter of Phoenix: Europa

Demeter: by her Zeus was father of Persephone

Leto: by her he was father of Apollo and Artemis

Satniois: the river runs westward from Mount Ida

Book XV   (The Pursuit back to the Ships)

Zeus awakens, angrily rebukes Hera, sends Iris to impose his will on Poseidon and sends Apollo to revive Hector so that he can drive the Greeks back to the ships. The Trojans advance, and Apollo fills in the trench and knocks down the wall. Hector is opposed by Ajax with Teucer, Menelaus and Antilochus. The Greeks are forced back to the ships. In stubborn defence Ajax leaps from ship to ship as the Trojans bring firebrands to Hector so that he can set fire to the ships.

NOTES AND GLOSSARY:

Hera fettered: the fettering of Hera is referred to by Zeus at the end of Book I. Nothing else is known about it

Heracles: Hera refers to the incident at XIV, 266

Hera's oath: she is almost telling the truth; see her words to Poseidon at VIII, 201–11 and his reply

Zeus's prediction: this summarises the rest of the poem, and goes on to relate Athene's part in the destruction of Troy. She provided the inspiration for the stratagem of the wooden horse

Themis: her name means 'law and custom'

Ascalaphus: his death is related at XIII, 518

the Furies: they avenge wrongs done to the family. In spite of Poseidon's account of the lottery, the older brother has the most power in heaven as on earth

Hector like a stallion: repeated from VI, 506–511 where it is applied to Paris

Apollo with the aegis: acts for Zeus who never appears in person on the battlefield

the palisade: a fence consisting of a row of stakes set firmly in the ground probably at the bottom of a trench

Patroclus and Eurypylus: the poet returns to the scene described at the end of Book XI

Antilochus's speech: he takes part in the foot-race in Book XXIII

Hector like fire: in his aristeia Hector is repeatedly associated with fire

Athene and Hector: the goddess actually plays a part in his death in Book XXII

Book XVI (The Deeds and Death of Patroclus)

Achilles yields to Patroclus's plea and lets him put on the armour of Achilles and lead the Myrmidons in battle. Achilles warns him not to pursue Hector. Patroclus inspires the Greeks and extinguishes the fire that had broken out on one of their ships. The Trojans retreat before his advance. Sarpedon offers resistance but is slain by Patroclus. Glaucus rallies Hector and the Trojans to recover the body of Sarpedon. Zeus spirits the body away to Lycia. Patroclus presses on, heedless of Achilles's warning. He is struck by Apollo, wounded by Euphorbus and finally killed by Hector whose death he predicts in his last words.

NOTES AND GLOSSARY:

Patroclus returns: he had been sent by Achilles in Book XI to find out which of the Greeks had been wounded

Patroclus's tears: repeated from IX, 14, relating to Agamemnon

Patroclus like a little girl: compare the simile of the child who builds sandcastles on the shore at XV, 362

Patroclus's reply: this recalls Nestor's speech at XI, 794–803

a prophecy: possibly referring to the two fates mentioned by Achilles at IX, 410

Achilles relents: in Book IX he had said he would wait until the Trojans reached his own ships. Even now he does not fight himself

Ajax at the ships: he fulfils his role as a dogged defender

Mount Pelion: in Thessaly not far from Phthia. Cheiron gave the spear to Peleus on his marriage to Thetis

Xanthus: sometimes translated as 'tawny'; Balius – 'dapple', Pedarus – 'jumper', Podargus – 'gleaming feet' or 'swift feet'. Horses were often said to be descended from winds (because of their speed). The horses had been given to Peleus by Poseidon as a wedding present

Eetion's city: see I, 366 and VI, 416

Spercheus: a river in Thessaly. Nothing is known of Achilles's sister

Achilles addresses his troops: reference is made here to the displeasure of the Myrmidons which is not described in the poem. This is unusual in Homer

Pelasgian Zeus: the Pelasgians were the earliest inhabitants of Greece who established the worship of Dodonian Zeus. Zeus had an oracle at Dodona in Epirus

Chimaera: the monster killed by Bellerophon and described at VI, 179–83

Patroclus pursues Hector: he is now going beyond what Achilles had ordered (see lines 83–96)

Zeus punishes human wickedness: this simile implies a more moral Zeus than he generally appears to be in the *Iliad*

Zeus and Sarpedon: this passage raises questions about the relationship between fate and the will of Zeus

the trace-horse: a third horse harnessed beside a pair to take the place of either of them in case of need. Pedarus is the mortal horse

the death of Sarpedon: Sarpedon is the first great hero to die. His death is marked like that of other great heroes by much divine interest and a death speech

Hector's taunt: this is of course not true. Achilles had expressly forbidden Patroclus to pursue Hector. The irony increases the dramatic effect

Patroclus's prophecy: this, and Hector's taunt, foreshadow the similar taunts and prophecy involving Achilles and Hector when Hector is slain in Book XXII

Book XVII   (The Aristeia of Menelaus)

The fight continues over the body of Patroclus. Menelaus kills Euphorbus but retreats before Ajax. Glaucus rebukes Hector who puts on Achilles's armour and encourages the Trojans. Ajax and Menelaus exhort the Greeks. The Trojans gain the body but are beaten off by Ajax. The battle continues until finally Menelaus and Meriones recover the body while the two Ajaces ward off the Trojans.

NOTES AND GLOSSARY:

Hyperenor: killed by Menelaus at XIV, 516

Menelaus in two minds: the Homeric heroes act not only upon impulse but with calculation

the dogs of Troy: decent burial was a matter of honour and piety, since it was believed that the soul of the departed could not pass to the underworld without it. Hence Zeus is concerned about the burial of his son Sarpedon (XVI, 667–75) and hence the particular horror of being exposed as carrion for dogs or crows (the idea recurs in the book, and with increasing emphasis, in the last third of the poem)

the lion veils his eyes: in order to avoid fear in the face of the huntsman's weapons. This legend persisted until Roman times

Sarpedon's body: Glaucus does not know that Zeus has spirited it away to Lycia. In the confusion of the fighting the heroes do not share the reader's knowledge of events

the armour of Achilles: a gift of the gods to Peleus at his marriage to Thetis (see XVIII, 84–5) and therefore presumably imperishable like the set of arms made for him, also in Book XVIII

wine at the public cost: this is the privilege of members of the council

mist spread by Zeus: compare XV, 668 and XVI, 567 where Zeus spreads night about the body of Sarpedon, thus adding to the confusion and danger. Compare also lines 366 and 644

the horses of Achilles: compare XIX, 404–17 where they speak

the rainbow: usually ominous in Homer (compare XI, 27)
Ajax prays for daylight: the final line of this prayer is a famous one
Menelaus sends a message to Achilles: Achilles has no armour now
  that Hector has despoiled Patroclus
the lion in retreat: repeated from XI, 550–55

Book XVIII   (The making of the Arms)

Antilochus brings news of Patroclus's death to Achilles. Thetis
hears Achilles's cries of despair and comes to him. He tells her that
he will rejoin the fighting. She promises to bring him new armour at
sunrise next day. Hector overtakes the Ajaces returning with the
body of Patroclus. Iris warns Achilles and he frightens off the
Trojans by appearing with the aegis which Athene has lent him.
Night falls. Hector rejects Polydamas's advice to withdraw into the
city. The Greeks grieve for Patroclus and wash his body. Thetis
prevails upon Hephaestus to make new armour for her son. There is
an elaborate description of the shield.

NOTES AND GLOSSARY:

Nereids: the daughters of Nereus, the old man of the sea.
  They are sea nymphs of the Mediterranean
Achilles's wish: that Peleus had married a mortal. He attributes
  his misfortunes to his divine parentage
Heracles: was deified after death, but Homer does not
  refer to this
Achilles has the aegis: to inspire terror; he is the only mortal to be
  lent armour by a divinity
the trumpet: not used in Homeric battles
Troy once rich: it is implied throughout the poem that Troy is a
  magnificent city, opulent and cultivated, so that
  the fall of Troy is the destruction of an ancient
  and cultivated civilisation
human sacrifice: this is carried out at XXI, 26
tripods with wheels: examples of these, of Phoenician craftsmanship,
  are known to have existed
Charis: this means 'grace'. The artificer needs grace to
  effect his art. In the *Odyssey* Hephaestus is married
  to Aphrodite
the crippled god: compare the story of his fall at I, 590–4, where he
  is thrown out by Zeus. The Greeks did not have a
  liberal attitude to physical deformity. Crippled
  infants were generally left in the open to die of
  exposure
Thetis and Peleus: there is legend that Zeus knew that Thetis was

	destined to bear a son who was stronger than his father, and therefore made sure that she married a mortal
the bellows:	they work by command from the god
the shield:	the pictures on the shield have no direct connection with the rest of the poem, and are not from heroic myth or legend. The use of metals of different kinds and colours and the art of inlaying bronze were well developed in Mycenaean times
Orion and the Bear:	in Northern Greece when Orion rises, the Bear is on the horizon from which he immediately ascends. As he is about to bathe in the ocean, the Bear is frightened by the presence of Orion the giant hunter
the trial:	it shows the beginnings of public justice and criminal law
the song of Linus:	usually said to be a dirge for the death of the young Linus, perhaps a personification of the spring or the summer
Daedalus:	the word means 'cunningly wrought' and is the name given to the artisan employed by the Cretan king Minos at Cnossus. He built the labyrinth, a maze in which the Minotaur was imprisoned. Ariadne was the daughter of Minos who helped Theseus escape from the labyrinth by means of a thread after he had killed the monstrous Minotaur
Ocean:	in Homer it encircles the world, and is therefore appropriately placed on the border of the shield

---

Book XIX   (The Renunciation of Anger)

Thetis brings the new armour to Achilles. Achilles summons an assembly and announces that he will end his feud with Agamemnon and return to the battlefield. Agamemnon publicly admits his folly and offers Achilles gifts and the return of Briseis. Achilles does not reject the offer but urges immediate engagement with the enemy. Odysseus insists upon feeding the troops first. The gifts and Briseis are brought forward. The troops eat, while Achilles abstains. Athene strengthens him with nectar. The Greeks assemble and Achilles arms. His horse Xanthus predicts his death.

NOTES AND GLOSSARY:

red nectar:	nectar is the wine of the gods, hence the adjective 'red'

this quarrel about a girl: here Briseis is again a mere chattel and spoil of war as she had been in the first book. In Book IX Achilles says that he loves her with all his heart (IX, 342–3), and Thetis tells Hephaestus that he missed her greatly (XVIII, 446). Here it is clear that whatever he felt for Briseis, he loved Patroclus with far deeper feeling. His death affects him more than would that of his father or his son (see lines 321–7)

Fate: the Homeric word is Moira which means 'portion' or 'lot'

Ate: a personification of folly or rashness

Alcmene and Hera: Hera is the goddess of childbirth

Eurystheus: not a son but a great-grandson of Zeus. His grandfather Perseus, who slew the Gorgon, was son of Zeus and Danae. Heracles performed his twelve labours at the command of Eurystheus

Agamemnon offers gifts: as a public recognition that he was in the wrong. For the same reason he speaks not only to Achilles but to the Greek assembly as a whole

Odysseus's speech: this insists on practicalities and formalities. In reply Achilles rejects both

Achilles recognises folly: in this short speech there seems to be an implied recognition of his own folly in the general statement. At any rate he accepts Agamemnon's apology

Briseis's lament: at IX, 336 Achilles calls Briseis his wife. It seems strange that the son of a goddess should marry a captive

hateful Helen: only here does any Greek speak ill of Helen

the son of Leto: Apollo (see XVI, 788–93)

the speaking horse: it is suggested that the Furies strike him dumb because the Furies overlook Destiny, and it is not the destiny of horses to speak

---

Book XX (The Battle of the Gods)

Zeus gives the gods permission to take sides in the war. Apollo in the guise of Lycaon urges Aeneas to confront Achilles. They meet and Aeneas is about to be killed when he is rescued by Poseidon. Achilles and Hector inspire their troops. Apollo warns Hector to avoid Achilles. Achilles kills numerous Trojans including Polydorus. Hector faces Achilles to avenge his brother. His spear-cast is deflected by Athene. Apollo snatches Hector away. Achilles continues the slaughter elsewhere.

NOTES AND GLOSSARY:

the rivers: it is not clear why all the rivers come to the council. In the next book Scamander takes part in the fighting

the nymphs: freshwater nymphs are Naiads, wood nymphs are Dryads

go beyond his destiny: Achilles is destined to fall before Troy

Callicolone: the name means 'beautiful hill'

Lyrnessus and Pedasus: towns in the Troad sacked by the Greeks before the siege of Troy

Heracles and the sea beast: Poseidon sent the sea beast to plague the Trojans because Laomedon (Priam's father and king of Troy) had cheated him and Apollo of their promised payment for building the walls of Troy (see XXI, 436–60). Heracles saved Hesione, Laomedon's daughter, from the clutches of the monster. Heracles was evidently aided by Athene who was not hostile to Troy until the judgment of Paris which came later

the genealogy of Aeneas: compare the similar speech of Glaucus to Diomedes in Book VI

the survival of Aeneas: Aeneas has a special destiny in Homer; he is to ensure the survival of the Dardan race. Later writers developed the story, notably the Roman poet Virgil (70–19BC) in the *Aeneid* in which Aeneas after the sack of Troy and the death of Priam leads the remnant of his people to Italy where his descendants found Rome

Helike: it is in the northern Peloponnese, and a notable centre of the cult of Poseidon

Achilles the runner: one of the special epithets of Achilles emphasises his swiftness of foot

Achilles the better man: Hector is not thinking of morals, but of the warrior's prowess. Possibly there is irony here

---

Book XXI   (The Battle by the River)

Achilles drives the Trojans to the river Scamander whose waters become choked with bodies. He kills Lycaon whom he had previously spared, and Asteropaeus, a descendant of a river god. As a descendant of Zeus, Achilles asserts the superiority of his ancestry. Scamander, already angry, rebukes Achilles and threatens to overwhelm him. In difficulties Achilles is rescued by Hera who commands Hephaestus, the fire god, to check Scamander. The gods then war among themselves. Ares, Aphrodite and Apollo, the supporters of Troy, are discomfited. Achilles chases the Trojans to the city but is distracted by Apollo taking the form of the Trojan Agenor.

NOTES AND GLOSSARY:

the captive youths: they are killed on the pyre of Patroclus at XXIII, 175

Lycaon: a foretaste of what is to come for Hector. The episode with the contrast of Achilles's earlier reprieve of Lycaon is designed to show his ruthlessness in the wake of the death of Patroclus

Jason's son: Euneus, king of Lemnos, an island in the Aegean sea. Jason was leader of the Argonauts who sailed in quest of the golden fleece

Imbros: an island near Troy

Arisba: on the coast of the Hellespont

Achilles's knees: Thetis likewise touches the knees of Zeus in the manner of a Greek suppliant (I, 512)

the breaking of bread: as if he had been a guest

Laothoe: Priam had fifty sons and therefore a number of wives. None of the Greeks in the poem seems to have been polygamous

Polydorus: he is killed at XX, 408–18

Achilles's reply: this is one of his most famous speeches, showing a ruthless fatalism

the bull sacrifice: rivers are frequently personified as bulls in Greek art. Scamander roars like a bull at line 237

Asteropaeus: he is related to a river, so that his death is an appropriate prelude to the fight with the river god

Paeonia: in Thrace

Achelous: a great river in Aetolia in north-western Greece

Scamander: he teaches Achilles that a mortal, even a descendant of Zeus, is no match for a god. Diomedes had wounded Ares and Aphrodite with the help of Athene

Apollo to Poseidon: men are like leaves; compare Glaucus at VI, 146. The gods who support Troy are well beaten in this scene, a portent of what is to come. Zeus is highly amused at the spectacle

Priam sees Achilles: Homer reintroduces Priam in preparation for the final scenes

Book XXII (The Death of Hector)

Hector, at the Scaean Gate, is entreated by Priam and Hecabe to enter the city. He determines to stand his ground, though when Achilles comes after him he flees and is chased around Troy three times. Zeus weighs their fates on his golden scales. Hector is doomed. Apollo deserts him; Athene comes to aid Achilles, taking the form of Deiphobus, Hector's brother, and induces Hector to face Achilles. In the fight Hector is killed, having predicted in his dying words the death of Achilles. Achilles, watched by Priam and Hecabe, ties Hector to his chariot and rides off dragging the body behind him. News reaches Andromache whose lamentation closes the book.

NOTES AND GLOSSARY:

Orion's dog: Sirius which rises at the height of the Mediterranean summer, hence the phrase 'dog days'

Lycaon and Polydorus: their deaths are related in earlier books

the snake: it was thought that the snake derived its poison from eating poisonous herbs

Polydamas: see his advice in XVIII, 249, which Hector ignored. He now regrets this and admits his weakness

Hector's shame: compare VI, 442, in his speech to Andromache

no ordinary race: a celebrated passage

Zeus grieves for Hector: as he had grieved for Sarpedon at XVI, 433–8. Athene's reply is similar to Hera's at lines 441–3

the golden scales: compare VIII, 69

Athene helps Achilles: she had helped Diomedes in Book V. Apollo helps to kill Patroclus, and Achilles will be killed by the arrows of Paris and Apollo. Mortal and immortal powers work hand in hand

Hector requests decent burial: compare a similar request and pledge when Hector faced Ajax at VII, 67–91. This is the customary chivalrous standard which Achilles will violate. It should be remembered that Hector had been eager to cut off the head of Patroclus at XVIII, 126

eat you raw: compare Hecabe's wish at XXIV, 212–13

Hector's prophecy: compare the prophecy of Patroclus at XVI, 854. He predicts the anger of the gods

Achilles abuses Hector's corpse: the poet refers to this act as shameful and outrageous

Astyanax fatherless: the lot of the fatherless in a patriarchal society was indeed difficult. For the reader who knows of

Astyanax's actual fate (to be thrown off the battlements of Troy) the passage is doubly pathetic. Homer makes no reference to this, but see Andromache's fear at XXIV, 734–6

Book XXIII   (Games for Patroclus)

Achilles continues to grieve. The ghost of Patroclus appears to him requesting burial for his body which is then burned on a great pyre with much ceremony. Funeral games, presided over by Achilles, are held in honour of Patroclus. There is a chariot race, a boxing match, wrestling, a foot-race, a combat with spears, discus-throwing, an archery contest, and finally spear-throwing. Prizes are awarded by Achilles to the successful competitors.

NOTES AND GLOSSARY:

cutting the hair: a sign of grief; compare line 135. The Greeks are 'longhaired'

the ghost of Patroclus: Homer's word is *psyche*. Patroclus makes it clear why proper burial is regarded as essential in Homer

the river: probably Styx

homicide: exile was the usual penalty

the ghost departs: gibbering, like a puff of smoke. Achilles refers to it as a likeness of the man without mind. This is the Homeric conception of the after-life, as a miserable existence in an insubstantial world

Spercheus: a river in Achilles's native Thessaly. The hair is probably associated with strength and here with survival. By cutting off the lock, Achilles accepts that he will not return home

the use of fat: for the practical purpose of ensuring that the corpse will burn

Aphrodite protects Hector: even the Greeks admire the marvellous beauty of Hector (XXII, 370); it is therefore appropriate that the goddess of beauty should preserve him

Ethiopian banquet: compare I, 423–4

breed of Tros: for their capture by Sthenelus, Diomedes's squire, see V, 321–4

Apollo helps Eumelus: because he had bred his horses

Achilles keeps the peace: there is a fine irony in Achilles's words and role here

the cuirass of Asteropaeus: captured at XXI, 183

Book XXIV   (The Ransoming of Hector)

Achilles continues to outrage the body of Hector. The gods take offence, and Zeus sends Thetis to tell Achilles to desist and accept a ransom. Zeus then sends Iris to Priam to tell him to go to Achilles with a ransom for Hector. Hecabe tries to dissuade him, but Priam sets off in the night and is met by Hermes disguised as a young Myrmidon prince who escorts him to the Greek camp. Achilles is moved by Priam's appeal and accepts the ransom. He urges Priam to eat with him and prepares sleeping quarters for him. Priam asks for a truce for burial which Achilles grants. He is warned by Hermes to return before dawn in case the other Greek leaders find him. Hermes escorts him back to Troy. Lamentations by Andromache, Hecabe and Helen are followed by the burial of Hector.

NOTES AND GLOSSARY:

Paris: he was shepherding his flocks on the slopes of Mount Ida when he was asked to make his judgment

Apollo condemns Achilles: for lacking shame or restraint. The key Homeric word is *aidos*

the Fates: probably the three fates, one of whom spins the thread, the second measures its length, and the third cuts it

the god's anger: from the Greek verb used here comes the noun 'nemesis'

Hera's reply: this is hardly concerned with the moral issue, merely with Achilles's status as the son of an immortal

Zeus's speech: Hector's piety is frequently remarked upon. Zeus's proposal for the ransom recognises that Achilles's honour must be protected. There must be gifts in exchange for the corpse. No mention of Priam is made to allow for the great astonishment felt by Achilles when Priam enters his tent

Troilus: famous in later legend, this is the only mention of him in the poem

Hermes's sandals and wand: his traditional attributes as guide and messenger. One of his functions was to escort the souls of the departed to Hades, so that he is closely associated with both sleep and death

Hermes meets Priam: they call one another father and son, appropriately, given the nature of Priam's appeal to Achilles. Hermes is disguised as a young

Myrmidon so that the scene subtly prepares us for the emotions of the actual meeting

Priam meets Achilles: he kisses the hand that has slain so many of his sons, a moment of dramatic climax fully appreciated by both the protagonists

Peleus: in a patriarchal society the bond between father and son is of central significance in a war-torn world

the jars of Zeus: a famous passage. Peleus and Priam experience a reversal of fortune, in Priam's case most thoroughly. Priam's realm extended well beyond the bounds of Troy, both inland and to neighbouring islands

Makar: this means 'happy' in Greek

Achilles invokes Patroclus: to apologise to him for allowing Hector's body to go for burial. He had vowed not to permit this at XXIII, 182–3

Niobe: she was turned into stone as a favour in answer to her own request. The gods rewarded her faithful grief. If Niobe took food, then so may Priam without the reproach that he lacks feeling

Sipylus: in Lydia, in Asia Minor

Part 3

Commentary

Structure and form

For the Greeks the epic was a long narrative poem to be distinguished from the lyric because it was not sung, and from the drama because it was not acted. The most famous remarks upon the form that have come down to us from antiquity are to be found in the *Poetics* of Aristotle (384–322BC), a fragmentary work most of which is about tragedy but in which there are incidental remarks about epic. For Aristotle, as for Greeks generally, Homer was the great genius of Greek literature. Although for him tragedy was a higher form than epic because of its greater economy of means and concentration of effect, Aristotle believed that the Homeric epics were perfect of their kind. Because of its scale an epic cannot have the unity of a tragedy; it is necessarily made up of parts that in themselves have a certain magnitude. Nevertheless Homer confines himself as far as is possible to the representation of a single action and achieves the greatest degree of unity possible in the epic form. On the matter of plot, Aristotle points out the simple truth that a plot does not have unity just because it deals with a single hero, for many diverse things may happen to an individual, and similarly an individual does many things which cannot possibly cohere in a single representation. The *Iliad* is not an *Achilleid*; it is not centred upon the life and character of Achilles. Indeed Achilles is absent from the poem from Book II until Book XVI except for Book IX and a brief appearance in Book XI. Similarly the *Odyssey* has as its unifying story not the life and character of Odysseus but his return home to Ithaca from Troy. Nor does the *Iliad* relate the whole of the Trojan War from beginning to end. Such a theme would have been too vast and overcomplicated by a variety of incidents weakly connected. Instead Homer chose one significant part of the war which is easily grasped as a whole, and is complete in itself, with a beginning, a middle and an end that are coherently linked by a chain of cause and effect, that is, one thing leading to another through probable or necessary consequences. Such is Aristotle's definition of a single action. Having decided upon his main action, Homer then used many episodes from the general story of the war, such as the catalogue of the ships in Book II, or the night attack in Book X, to diversify and enrich his poem (see *Poetics*, XXIII and XXIV).

The main action of the *Iliad* has to do with the anger of Achilles. Slighted by Agamemnon in a quarrel, Achilles angrily withdraws from the fighting and asks his goddess mother Thetis to persuade Zeus to give the Trojans success so that the Greeks will be forced to recognise his worth (Book I). Zeus acts upon his promise, and the leading Greeks are wounded (Book XI). With the Greeks in danger of defeat, his friend Patroclus persuades Achilles to allow him to fight wearing his armour. Patroclus is subsequently killed by Hector (Book XVI). Stung by grief and remorse Achilles returns to the battle to avenge his friend. He kills Hector in single combat and drags off his corpse fixed to his chariot (Book XXII). The dreadful consequences of his anger to himself and to others are shown in full. These four books (I, XI, XVI, and XXII) contain the main action and what may be called the irreducible plot of the *Iliad*. There is a clearly discernible chain of cause and effect both in the actions of the gods (who accept the rulings of Fate) and in the actions and characters of men bringing about certain natural or probable consequences, leading inexorably to the death of Hector and the climax of the poem. In comparison to the *Odyssey* with its complex plot involving reversal through disguise and discovery, Aristotle remarks that the plot of the *Iliad* is simple (*Poetics* XXIV, I). Homer might have complicated his plot by making Hector believe that Patroclus in Achilles's armour was Achilles himself, but he chose not to do so. Whereas the *Odyssey* is 'ethical' and turns on character, on the manifestation of various aspects of Odysseus's character which are put to the test in many different circumstances, the *Iliad* is 'pathetic', variously interpreted as based on passion or involving calamity. Both interpretations apply; the passion (the *menis* or anger which is the first word of the poem) causes the calamity, the death of Patroclus, the pivot upon which the action turns.

While there is a simple single action in the *Iliad*, the great art of the poet is apparent in the skill with which the main plot is expanded. The scope of the poem is immediately widened so that it is not confined to the anger of Achilles, but becomes truly an *Iliad*, that is a poem embracing the whole Trojan story (Ilium being another name for Troy). In Book I the request of Thetis that Zeus aid her son becomes the will of Zeus, and in the opening of Book II Zeus begins to act upon his promise by sending a false dream to Agamemnon. This has the effect of starting the fighting, but it does not immediately result in Trojan success. The first day's battle after the resumption of fighting in Book II is inconclusive and little happens to advance the plan until Zeus reasserts himself in Book VIII. The main function of the first day's activity (Books II–VII) is twofold: the protagonists on both sides are introduced and the general context in which the main action takes place is revealed.

Book II explores the unstable situation in the Greek camp dramatised in the folly of Agamemnon's test and the subsequent flight of the army. The temperamental instability of Agamemnon, his inept leadership and the role of Nestor as the experienced old sage (all apparent in the quarrel scene of the opening book) are further confirmed and Odysseus is introduced as a self-possessed, wily and capable character in direct contrast to Agamemnon and in indirect contrast to Achilles. The council in which Thersites rails against Agamemnon, besides being of great dramatic interest in itself, re-enacts the quarrel scene of Book I with Agamemnon again maligned. Finally the catalogue of forces widens the scale of the poem from a quarrel between a few individuals to involve the whole Mediterranean world.

In Book III the scene changes to Troy and establishes both the main Trojan characters and the current climate of feeling in the city. At the same time the action involving Paris, Helen and Menelaus and the presence of Aphrodite puts before us the protagonists of the original quarrel and indirectly recounts the causes of the war. In Hector and Paris we have two contrasting characters, one dutiful, the other pleasure-loving. The scene between Priam and Helen gives brief character sketches of the Greeks and also establishes the peerless beauty of Helen and her comparative innocence in Trojan eyes. Paris is the guilty party, an inference further confirmed by his defeat in the duel. The superiority of Menelaus over Paris and that of Ajax over Hector in the duels of Books III and VII suggest Trojan inferiority even without Achilles. The breaking of the truce by Pandarus is an act of treachery paralleling the original duplicity of Paris. Later the refusal of Paris to give up Helen in Book VII suggests the impasse which had led to the war.

While the first Trojan scene recalls the past, the second major Trojan scene in Book VI looks ominously to the future. The parting of Hector and Andromache firmly establishes Hector as the mainstay of the Trojan cause upon whom all will depend and is full of foreboding for his fate and that of the city with which he is identified. Between the Trojan scenes the main event is the aristeia of Diomedes in Book V. Again we are reminded that even without Achilles the Greeks have great fighters, and Diomedes's success is a fitting prelude to the Trojan fears that follow in Book VI.

The expansion of the plot could have been accomplished by a retrospective narrative by one of the characters of events leading up to the present. In the *Odyssey*, Odysseus tells his past adventures to the King of the Phaeacians in an after-dinner speech (Books IX to XII), but in the *Iliad* Homer fills in the past and broadens the scope of his poem without relinquishing his present narrative. In fact the past becomes a cause of dramatic interest in the present, in the duel between Paris and Menelaus for example. The past is incorporated indirectly into the present with no sacrifice of immediacy or dramatic tension. What is perhaps sacrificed is some measure of probability. Strictly speaking it is improbable that the warring parties would agree to a duel to settle all after a nine-year siege. We may feel that Priam should be able to recognise his principal opponents, and that it might have occurred to the Greeks to protect their ships with a wall earlier in the campaign. Homer's method results too in incongruities. It has often been pointed out that the catalogue of ships is a more appropriate account of their assembly at Aulis where the Greeks had gathered to sail in the first place. But though the main action of the poem is entirely probable and satisfactorily linked together by a chain of cause and effect, the *Iliad* is not constructed like a naturalistic novel of the nineteenth century. Homer's primary concern is the continuously unfolding drama of the immediate present.

The main action of the irreducible plot is first diversified and enriched by the various episodes in Books II to VII which widen the scope of the poem to embrace the whole Trojan war. The second expansion of the irreducible plot is the skilful prolongation and retardation of the action in which Zeus carries out his plan to give the Trojans success so that the Greeks will appreciate the worth of Achilles. Book XI contains all that is strictly necessary for this phase of the irreducible plot, but the action is prolonged from Book VIII to Book XV, principally by two simple devices. The will of Zeus is thwarted by the activities of other gods, and in the human sphere of military tactics the Trojan advance takes place by stages involving the capture of the central ground (Book VIII), the breach of the wall (Book XII) and the arrival at the ships (Book XV). In the first day's fighting (Books II–VII) Zeus does not act decisively; he sends the dream to Agamemnon and instructs Athene to cause Pandarus to break the truce, but other actions of the gods influence the course of events, notably the support of Athene for Diomedes. In the second day's fighting (Book VIII) Zeus decides to bring matters to a head and forbids the other Olympians to take part in the war. The Trojans have considerable success and are able to camp on the Trojan plain. This Greek reverse leads to the embassy to Achilles, and to the plan to reconnoitre the Trojan camp by night (Books IX and X). The course of the action is not directly affected by the embassy or by the night expedition so that the third day's fighting continues where the second left off. Zeus allows Agamemnon some early reward but promises Hector success until sunset. The leading Greeks, Agamemnon, Odysseus and Diomedes, are then wounded, and Ajax is forced to retire (Book XI). The action is prolonged in the next book by the fight at the wall which the Greeks have built to protect their ships (Book

XII). In the next two books (XIII and XIV) the action slows down when Zeus later takes his eye off the fighting, thus enabling Poseidon to encourage the Greeks, and when he is lulled to sleep by Hera. In Book XV Zeus awakes and Trojan fortunes are restored, and some slight advance is made upon the state of events at the end of Book XII in that the Trojans are not only through the wall but threaten the ships themselves. This brings us to the pivotal turn in the action with the deaths of Sarpedon and Patroclus in Book XVI.

At the pivotal point two thirds of the way through the narrative, the poet has managed to expand and diversify the irreducible plot without losing sight of it, and without allowing any of the episodes to acquire undue significance. Because everything is narrated in the present tense, there is, generally speaking, the illusion of vigorous forward movement, but in reality most of what happens before Book XVI is inconclusive and inconsequential, in that the main action is not seriously affected. The flight of the army, the inconclusive duel between Menelaus and Paris, the truce made and broken, the aristeia of Diomedes that ends in an exchange of gifts, the inconclusive duel of Hector and Ajax, the building of the wall that is later breached, even the embassy to Achilles, the night attack, the aristeia of Agamemnon that ends in his being wounded, the intervention of Poseidon, the aristeia of Idomeneus broken off because he is too weary to continue, the intervention of Hera and the wounding of Hector – all these actions serve to extend and interrupt the main action, but no one of them is allowed significantly to develop to a point where it threatens to complicate the essential simplicity of the main action that constitutes the irreducible plot.

Furthermore the narrative skill of the poet is apparent in the gradual build-up to the pivotal action of Book XVI. The death of Sarpedon which is to motivate Hector to pursue Patroclus is the first death of significance, artistically speaking, in the *Iliad*. It is marked by unusual divine interest; Zeus actually contemplates suspending fate for the sake of his beloved son. In all the fighting prior to Book XVI there are no significant scenes of pathos involving a major hero, and Sarpedon is the first figure to be given a death speech of some length. The deaths of Sarpedon and Patroclus provide material of importance for repetition and variation in the later narrative of the death of Hector, but they do not simply offer repetition of what has gone before in the poem.

There is a gradual building up to the pivotal calamity whence the poem moves much more directly to its climax. The irreducible plot could be expanded equally well after the pivotal turn as before, but there is no artistic reason for significant delay after the calamity. The proportions of two thirds before the pivotal calamity and one third following it is a satisfying structure, and reflects the stubborn persistence of Achilles's angry withdrawal, and the rapidity with which events take their necessary course after Achilles's return. From the death of Patroclus to the death of Hector and the close of the poem the narrative is carefully paced, with each stage contributing to the cumulative effect.

The struggle over Patroclus's body in Book XVII follows naturally from his death and dramatises the concern for the proper treatment of the dead which is to be a major factor at the close of the poem when Achilles abuses the corpse of Hector. The episode in which Hephaestus makes arms for Achilles (in Book XVIII) is well integrated into the main action since Nestor in Book XI suggests to Patroclus that he fight in Achilles's armour. When Hector despoils Patroclus's corpse, Achilles is in need of a new set of armour now provided by the gods. The pause in the action here is natural, artistically and logically. The narrative of the third day's fighting has been continuous, stretching over seven books. This is an ideal moment for an interlude which takes us beyond the narrow focus of the fighting on the plain of Troy. In Book XIX comes Achilles's reconciliation with the Greeks, followed by preparations for the final day's fighting. In the argument over whether they should first take food, Odysseus points out that the meal is a practical necessity, but the taking and sharing of food, from which Achilles here abstains, is given a symbolic significance that will be apparent again in the final book when Achilles persuades Priam to eat. In Book XX, Achilles's ruthless fighting power is established. There is some slowing down which intensifies suspense when Hector, who faces Achilles when the latter kills his brother Polydorus, is whisked away by Poseidon. In Book XXI, Achilles's power and stature are made more formidable in the fight with the river god. After the death of Hector in Book XXII, the episode of the games in Book XXIII is of course superfluous to the main action but it arises naturally from it, providing a release of tension and change of mood after the fighting of the previous day and before the solemn proceedings of the final book in which the anger is finally resolved.

The construction of the poem, therefore, however loose and elastic it may appear, is carefully plotted. The single simple action which gives the poem unity is expanded, prolonged and retarded, and paced with care to give maximum impact first to the pivotal calamity and thereafter to the climax and its aftermath at the end. Everything expresses the one intention and contributes in Aristotle's phrase to one result, one end (*Poetics*, XXIII, 1–2).

Apart from essential unity of action, the *Iliad* also has unity of place; all the human action is concentrated in one small area embracing the Greek camp, the Trojan plain and the city itself. Finally there is a remarkable concentration of time. The scale of the poem, its episodic nature and the apparently leisurely pace of the narrative are such that, paradoxically, it is possible to underestimate the tight and careful concentration of events into such a brief space of time. It may seem that Zeus has forgotten his promise, but in reality only one day passes before he takes vigorous action to carry it out, and only five days pass between the appeal of Thetis to Zeus in Book I and the death of Hector in Book XXII. Allowing for a day's inactivity while both sides bury their dead, Achilles is absent from the fighting for just three days.

So concentrated is the *Iliad* that its whole action takes place in a mere fifty days. Of these twenty-two pass in Book I. The plague rages for nine days and on the tenth Achilles calls a council. After the quarrel, Thetis promises to petition Zeus when the gods return after eleven days' feasting with the Ethiopians. A further twenty-two days pass in the last book. For eleven days Achilles regularly abuses the corpse of Hector. On the twelfth, the gods command him to desist. That night Priam comes to Achilles with a ransom. Achilles allows Priam a truce for the burial of Hector. The Trojans prepare for nine days and bury Hector on the tenth. The intervening events (from the end of the first book to the beginning of the last) take place in the course of six days.

After Achilles's withdrawal the first day's fighting takes us from Book II to the duel of Hector and Ajax in Book VII. A day is then taken for the burial of the dead. On the next day Zeus acts vigorously on his promise to Thetis (Book VIII). After the events of the night, described in Books IX–X, the longest section of the narrative covers the third day's fighting. Zeus promises Hector success until sunset. Hector kills Patroclus and after the struggle over his body, news of his death is brought to Achilles (Books XI–XVIII). The fourth day's fighting sees the return of Achilles and culminates in the death of Hector (Books XIX–XXII). On the following day Patroclus is buried (Book XXIII). Six days pass altogether, four days of fighting, two of burial.

The simple economy and clarity of design are apparent in the use made of intervening evenings and nights. Each is the occasion of some addition to the plot. Agamemnon's dream precedes the first day's fighting, and at the end of it councils take place in both camps, as well as negotiations for the burial of the dead. During the following evening and night the Greeks build the wall (Book VII). The next evening the embassy to Achilles occurs (Book IX), followed by the reconnoitre of the Trojan camp (Book X). During the next night the Greeks mourn Patroclus, while Hephaestus makes new armour for Achilles (Book XVIII). After Hector's death, there is an evening council in the Greek camp and a meal. The ghost of Patroclus appears to Achilles (Book XXIII). Priam visits the tent of Achilles at night (Book XXIV).

This simple overall concentration of time and the overall unity of place are a consequence of the general poetic design, concentrating upon one single action. This action is diversified, extended and enriched by many episodes but the essential unity is not broken. The episodes do not extend the action to places far away from the plain of Troy, nor do they extend the temporal framework in which the main action takes place. Herein lies a simple source of the peculiar concentration and intensity of the *Iliad*. The main action of the irreducible plot of the *Iliad* in comparison to the subjects of other great epics is insignificant in itself. The essential subject of the *Odyssey*, the journey home, has grandeur of its own. In the *Aeneid* of the Roman poet Virgil (70–19BC), the essential subject is again a momentous one, of a journey and a struggle which are to make possible a great new civilisation. In *Paradise Lost* of John Milton (1608–74), the grand English epic constructed on Classical principles, the subject is no less than the Fall of Man. Against these the anger of Achilles is in itself trivial, yet, paradoxically perhaps, no other epic has quite the scale of the *Iliad*, since scale is not something intrinsic to the subject of a poem, but is a consequence of the poet's concentrated presentation of that subject. Nobody can believe after experiencing the *Iliad* that the anger of Achilles is a trivial thing.

There are two further features of the *Iliad* that contribute to the concentrated effect of the poem, adding both structural unity and scale. The first concerns the use made of the Olympian deities, the 'divine machinery' of the poem. In the quarrelsome episodes on Olympus and in some of their interventions on the battlefield, Homer's anthropomorphic gods and goddesses diversify the main action by introducing comedy into the poem. In Book I, after the seriousness of the quarrel between Agamemnon and Achilles, the quarrel between husband and wife on Olympus is presented in an altogether lighter vein. That the most powerful of the gods and their king should also be a hen-pecked husband is an amusing incongruity. At the same time the absurdities of the gods are sometimes a counterpoint to the seriousness of what happens in the mortal sphere; their inconsequential wounds and quarrels seem trivial in comparison to the serious wounds and quarrels of those who are subject to death. The intervention of the gods can also serve to magnify the significance of human actions. But whatever else may be said of the Homeric gods, they are a convenient structural device; hence the term 'divine machinery'. The central action of the poem turns on the will of Zeus, on his promise to Thetis that the Trojans will succeed until the Greeks are forced to appreciate Achilles's worth. Every action is initiated by a god. Apollo sends the plague at the beginning of the poem. In the first day's fighting (Books II–VII) the various gods give their support to their favourites. On the second day (Book VIII) Zeus acts more decisively on his promise and forbids the other gods to participate. In the third day's fighting (Books XI–XVII) Zeus promises Hector success until sunset. When he takes his eye off the fighting Poseidon intervenes and Zeus is then lulled to sleep by Hera. On the fourth day after the return of Achilles (Books XIX–XXII), the gods are allowed to take sides to make the contest more even for a while until the gods supporting Troy are defeated by those encouraging the Greeks, and divine aid for Hector is withdrawn. Finally the close of the poem is brought about by the displeasure of Zeus who forbids Achilles to continue abusing the corpse of Hector.

Related to this use of the divine machinery is the prophecy of future made by both gods and mortals. A prediction or foreboding has its particular local dramatic function, but the use of prophecy is also a means by which the poet reveals the structure of his poem and exerts his control over the narrative.

In the earlier part of the poem the prophecies are expressed in general terms. Thetis refers generally to the doom of Achilles when talking to her son (I, 416–17). Agamemnon's instinct tells him that Troy will fall (IV, 163–5). In Book VI the fate of Troy is identified with Hector, its chief defender. Andromache fears for her husband's safety, and Hector has the same prophetic instinct as Agamemnon (VI, 448–9), fearing for the city, its inhabitants, and ·chiefly for Andromache. The *Iliad* is narrated in the eternal present, but just as the past determines the structure of the present most obviously for Paris, Helen and Menelaus, so the future weighs heavily on the present for Achilles, Hector and Andromache. Just before the pivotal calamity, Zeus, who has not revealed the future so fully before, predicts not only the whole future course of the *Iliad* but also the future doom of Troy itself (XV, 59–77). Thereafter at crucial moments in the last eight books, Homer uses specific prophecy for dramatic effect. The narrator predicts Hector's doom at the moment when he puts on Achilles's helmet (XVI, 799–80). In Hector's moment of triumph, the dying Patroclus predicts his death (XVI, 852–4). Speaking to her son, Thetis confirms that his death will follow closely upon that of Hector (XVIII, 95–6). Achilles's death is further predicted by his horse Xanthus (XIX, 409–10), by Achilles himself in reply (XIX, 421) and in more specific detail by the dying Hector (XXII, 359–60). The future doom of the Trojans figures prominently in the pleas made by Priam and Hecabe to Hector just before the final combat, and also in the conversation between Priam and Achilles and in the lamentations with which the poem closes. Besides having pathetic or ironic effect at the moment of utterance, all these prophecies together propel the narrative towards its conclusion, while at the same time they suggest the workings of an inescapable destiny that is gradually being brought to pass through the apparently random chaos of present events.

Such is the scale of the poem that we may from time to time lose sight of the whole in the general flux of the fighting and miss the general direction of events. Decisive prophecies and divine inter-ventions make the narrative outlines clear. If there were too few of them, the overall structure of events might not be clear, while if there were too many of them the sense of inevitable fate would be oppressive and would diminish the apparent freedom of the protagonists in the present action. Whether the inevitable fate is to be identified with the will of Zeus or whether the will of Zeus is simply an expression of a fate which binds gods and mortals alike matters little. When Zeus puts the fates of Hector and Achilles on the scales (XXII, 209–13) the result is the same whatever interpretation is put upon the workings that bring it about. Such use of the divine machinery may be said to fulfil two related functions; in the first place, artistic cohesion is given to the poem, and in the second, the Greek sense of fate and its workings is given concrete and dramatic expression.

Despite the many problems posed by discrepancies and inconsistencies (these have been ignored here, but some of them will be listed in Part 4) the overall design of the *Iliad* is remarkably unified, and it is this argument based on its design that has proved persuasive to those who believe in the essential unity of authorship in the *Iliad*. At any rate the unified and concentrated design of the *Iliad* has always been regarded as characteristically Greek. The *Iliad* because of its very nature as a long narrative poem has not the concentration of the tragedy *King Oedipus* by Sophocles (c.496–406BC) upon which Aristotle is thought to have based his famous analysis of tragedy in the *Poetics*. But the concentration of Classical epic will be apparent when the *Iliad* is contrasted with a loosely constructed romantic tragedy such as *Antony and Cleopatra* of Shakespeare (1564–1616), which is episodic in its action, takes place in several places spread over two continents and extends over a period lasting several years. The subordination of the parts to the whole and the concern for overall unity, clarity and simplicity of design are major principles of Classical art. In architecture these principles and tendencies find their perfect expression in a Classical Greek temple such as the Parthenon built on the Athenian Acropolis in the age of Pericles, the famous leader of Athens in the mid-fifth century BC when Athenian power and culture were at their peak of influence and achievement. The design and decoration of individual features of the ideal Greek temple are so controlled that no one part is disproportionate but each contributes to the overall harmony and symmetry of the whole. Here an obvious contrast might be a Gothic cathedral which is inspired by a quite different ideal and aspiration.

The Homeric poems are the earliest documents of Greek civilisation that have survived; nevertheless their design is the expression of a mature art. Their influence on the subsequent course of Greek culture is incalculable. The aesthetic principles underlying Aristotle's critical analysis of Greek literature in the fourth century have their origin in the creative achievement of the Homeric poems composed centuries earlier.

The heroic world: attitudes and values

Historians of Greek culture have often remarked that Homer was the Bible of the Greeks, meaning by this not only that the Homeric poems occupied the same central position in Greek education and life that the Bible has had in Judaeo-Christian culture, but also that the Homeric poems are a classic expression of the Hellenic spirit as the Bible is the great record of Jewish experience and the Hebraic spirit.

The Hebraic and Hellenic images of man differ fundamentally. In the Old Testament, man is created in the image of God. The Old Testament God is remote and mysterious and works through the Spirit. He is a stern and jealous God who demands of his chosen people that they should obey His commandments and live a righteous life. Sinful man looks to the coming of the Kingdom of God and lives in fear and trembling of God's judgment in this life and in the world to come. The Homeric gods are created in man's image and are neither remote nor mysterious. They are given human form and are fully anthropomorphic beings, sharing the passions, the quarrelsomeness and the vanity of man. They enjoy the feast and have little concern with the moral or spiritual life. Although there are occasional signs that Zeus is angered by human wickedness (XVI, 386–93), the gods are characteristically amoral and intervene in the affairs of men capriciously according to their own private and conflicting whims. Troy does not fall because of the anger of Zeus. Zeus has no quarrel with the Trojans who are one of his favourite peoples. Nor does Homeric man seek to live a righteous life in the knowledge of judgment to come; rather he seeks glory here and now and the fame of it in future time. As he is about to meet his doom, Hector hopes to die gloriously while performing an heroic act that will reach the ears of men in years to come (XXII, 304–5). In the Homeric after-life in Hades what survives is a mere likeness or semblance of the true bodily self

(XXIII, 99-107). The essential reality is physical consciousness.

With neither the reward of Heaven nor the pains of Hell to look forward to, Homeric man seeks to make the most of his present existence in the material world. Few poems have so celebrated the vitality of immediate physical life and 'the body's fervour'.

The primacy of the physical nature is reinforced by the imagery of the many similes in which men and gods are compared to inanimate forces and to animal nature itself. Here it is the power of natural forces whether in the elements or in the animal kingdom that predominates. Nature is not humanised or sentimentalised. Instead human nature is identified with a natural order of things greater and more powerful than man.

In a poem in which the world is at war it is to be expected that human worth should be reckoned by the standards of the warrior. In the quarrel old Nestor reminds Agamemnon and Achilles that he has known very much better men than they are, and it is clear that he means that the heroes of old were capable of greater physical prowess (I, 256–66). Achilles owes his stature among the Greeks at Troy to the achievements of his own right arm and his swiftness of foot. When he rejects the pleas of Lycaon for mercy, he reminds Lycaon that Patroclus has died who was a better man than he by far. Death will come even to Achilles who is beautiful and mighty and born of a goddess (XXI, 107–13). Achilles measures his own worth here in strictly physical terms. Hector admits the superiority of Achilles (XX, 434) and in the final confrontation Achilles tells Hector to stand his ground and prove his worth as a soldier (XXII, 268–9).

In the fight the heroes experience a surge of *menos*, of fierceness and strength, a word used also of lions and wild boars. This is necessary to sustain the great physical exertions of the heroes that follow one upon another. Although Homer has no word for reason, he does have words for thought and reflection. But when the heroes are propelled into action what usually motivates them is a feeling in the blood, *thumos*. Many of Homer's words do not bear very exact resemblances to the English words used to translate them. *Thumos*, which seems to be related to the Greek verb meaning 'to rush along', is what causes strong feeling or passion. It is associated with natural strength, the heart, desire, and appetite for food. It has to do with man's basic inner nature which for Homer is physical. To Andromache's plea that he refrain from fighting, Hector says that he would feel shame before the Trojan women if he did not join battle. But he also says that his *thumos* compels him to fight (VI, 441–6). However terrible the consequences, the heroes experience compulsion from within, so that the battles are whole-hearted and there is exhilaration in the fighting. Homer uses the word *charma* to express eagerness for battle and joy in the fight. When

Apollo breathes *menos* into Hector, the Trojan leader is likened to a stallion who has broken loose and is galloping off joyfully to his favourite pastures confident in his own splendour (XV, 263–8). As he directs the fight, Zeus similarly glories in his own strength and power.

It is not only in the fighting that we are conscious of the physical world in Homer. There is much eating and drinking and talk of the feast amongst men and gods. For the gods life is an eternal banquet. Thetis tells Achilles that the gods are away in Ethiopia feasting and will not be back for twelve days (I, 423–5). When the Greeks restore Chryseis, a sacrifice and a merry meal are described in detail (I, 457–74). At the end of Book I, Hephaestus reminds Zeus and Hera that their quarrelling over the foolish race of man threatens to spoil their pleasure in the feast (I, 573–9). The gods are reconciled and drink to their hearts' content. After the first day's fighting there is a meal in the Greek camp at which Ajax is rewarded with the best portion of beef (VII, 313–20). Not all the descriptions of food and its preparation are formulaic or perfunctory. Nestor provides Patroclus with a wine which has been laced with onion, honey, barley and goat's milk cheese (XI, 629–41). In all such passages there is realistic detail: Homer dwells on concrete particulars which are clearly and simply represented.

In the representation of the physical world, Homer celebrates physical beauty in persons and material objects. In the descriptions of persons there are many details, usually in the comments of others, that enhance the beauty and dignity of the protagonists. Hector remarks sarcastically upon Paris's good looks and fine hair (III, 55). Helen's beauty is such that the Trojan elders cannot blame the Greeks and Trojans for fighting over her (III, 156–8). Briseis is like golden Aphrodite (XIX, 282). When Hector is finally dead, the Greeks marvel at the size and beauty of his body (XXII, 370–1). After they have eaten, Priam expresses his wonder at the stature and beauty of Achilles who is the very image of a god. Achilles in turn admires the appearance of Priam (XXIV, 629–33). Heroic excellence is manifested in perfection of physical form. Moral deformity is expressed in physical ugliness as in the case of Thersites who is crook-backed, bald and lame (II, 216–19). The value set upon beauty is apparent in the fate of the godlike Ganymede, a mortal who grew to be the most beautiful youth in the world and because of his good looks was stolen by the gods to be cupbearer to Zeus (XX, 232–5). The gods themselves protect the bodies of their favourites Sarpedon, Patroclus and Hector from decay. Their own beauty is taken for granted, and constantly implied by the use of recurring adjectives, for example, golden Aphrodite and Thetis of the silver feet. The most famous Greek sculptor of the fifth century BC is said to have been inspired by the majestic description of the dark eyebrows and ambrosial locks of Zeus at I, 528–9 when he made his famous statue of Zeus at Olympia. The description of the messenger of the gods, Hermes, at XXIV, 339–48 with his golden sandals and wand, 'looking like a princely youth at the most graceful time when the beard first begins to grow' fits exactly his representation in the statues of later time.

The beauty and excellence of physical objects are everywhere apparent in the descriptions of armour, not only the armour of Achilles (in Book XVIII) but also the shield of Ajax (VII, 219–23) and the armour of Agamemnon (XI, 15–46). The beauty of such objects is both decorative and functional. The arms are finely made, beautifully and appropriately decorated and excellent of their kind. Extended descriptions of material objects usually have an ulterior function. The history of Agamemnon's sceptre which once belonged to Zeus is told in such a way as to enhance his power and authority (II, 100–9). Nestor's cup is so heavy when full that only a man of unusual strength can lift it (XI, 629–37). Heroic values are apparent in these descriptions. The beauty of Aeneas's horses of divine descent (V, 218–28) and of the horses of the Thracian Rhesus which are much admired by the Greeks (X, 526–65) is expressed chiefly in their speed which enables their owners to outrun all rivals.

Possessions, prizes and gifts are valued in themselves but also for the distinction and honour they convey. This is also true of spoils taken from a defeated foe. It is because material possessions and prizes are a sign of the esteem in which the possessor is regarded that Achilles is so angered when Agamemnon takes his prize in the opening quarrel. Although Achilles later claims to love Briseis (IX, 342–3), in the quarrel itself and when the quarrel is mended Briseis is regarded as a mere chattel (I, 185). In depriving Achilles of her, Agamemnon dishonours him and threatens the whole basis upon which relations are constructed in the Homeric world. Honour, pride, status and self-esteem (all that is contained in the Greek word *time*) are determining factors in relations between men, between gods, and between men and gods. Apollo's honour is affected when Agamemnon dishonours his priest. When Thetis appeals to Zeus to aid her son, she says that she will be the least honoured of the Olympians if he denies her request (I, 516). In many instances (for example IX, 533–7) mortals incur the wrath of gods because sacrifices have been neglected. Conversely Zeus feels well-disposed towards the Trojans and Hector because they have been generous in their offerings to him (IV, 43–9; XXII, 168–72; XXIV, 66–70). Excellence must have due recognition and honour. The honour of the gods is respected when proper sacrifices are made; the honour of men is evident in material possessions.

The beauty of persons and of material objects is simply an aspect of heroic life where excellence is the norm. The Homeric hero consciously endeavours to excel. Speaking to Diomedes, the Lycian Glaucus tells him that his father sent him to Troy with the advice always to excel over the rest and not to shame his forebears who were the best in Lycia (VI, 208–10). Nestor later tells Patroclus that when he had recruited Achilles for the Trojan expedition, the latter's father, Peleus, had told his son always to strive to outdo the others (XI, 784). Hector's hope for his son Astyanax is that in future time men will say 'He is better than his father' as he returns from the battlefield bearing the blood-stained armour of his foe (VI, 479–81). The supreme test for the Homeric hero is, of course, the battlefield; this is where he will prove his excellence. But the desire to excel and the emphasis upon excellence are apparent throughout the poem, for instance, in the competitive spirit of the games in Book XXIII where the competition for glittering prizes is as intense as it is on the battlefield, even if the stakes are not so high (compare XXII, 157–61).

The promptings of the heroic spirit are most clearly articulated in the famous speech of Sarpedon in Book XII (lines 310–28). Sarpedon asks Glaucus why they are singled out for honour at the feast with special seats and the best food and drink among the Lycians who look upon them as gods. Why do they have the best land with orchards and wheatfields? Their social position obliges them to lead the Lycians in fighting so that their followers will acknowledge that they earn their privileges by virtue of their great prowess on the battlefield. At the same time Sarpedon says that if they could actually be like gods and avoid old age and death he would not urge Glaucus to join the fight where glory is gained. The Homeric adjective 'bringing glory' fits the context well. Elsewhere Homer uses many adjectives that express the grisliness of the fight. But since they cannot escape death in its countless forms, Sarpedon urges that they join the fight and either gain honour for themselves or give it to others. The heroic resolve is the conscious choice to risk a glorious death rather than to forego glory for the sake of holding onto an insignificant life (compare the choice of Achilles at IX, 410–16).

The heroes of the *Iliad* therefore live what is on their terms a fully heroic life. There is consciousness of an heroic past in the nostalgia of the old soldier Nestor for past campaigns (see for example XI, 670–762) and in Agamemnon's account of the great expedition of the previous generation of heroes against Thebes (IV, 372–99). But the heroes of the present campaign are conscious of their own worth and fully confident of their superior strength. To Agamemnon's taunt that Diomedes is not as good a fighter as his father Tydeus, Sthenelus, the squire of Diomedes, confidently asserts that the present generation of fighters are better than their fathers by far (IV, 404–10). The

Odyssey by contrast is set in a post-heroic world; all the heroes of the Trojan War look back with nostalgia to an heroic past from the standpoint of a meaner domestic present.

Despite the compelling desire to excel and the intense regard that the Homeric hero has for his honour and self-esteem, the heroes are not an unscrupulous breed of supermen who have no regard for right and wrong and no sense of decency and decorum. In fact the contrary is the case. The converse of the great sense of honour felt by the heroes is the sense of shame expressed by Hector in Book VI. The Homeric word *aidos* is the restraining influence that on the one hand prevents cowardice and on the other prevents the concern for honour growing into overweening pride and arrogance. Included in the concept of *aidos* is reverence due to the gods, to elders, and to the dead.

Implied in the Homeric word *themis* are codes of conduct that have been sanctioned by tradition. As the most powerful king, Agamemnon is privileged to test the army (II, 73) but custom allows Nestor to speak up against his folly (II, 337–68). In the council in Book IX, Diomedes uses the privilege of freedom of speech in open council to criticise Agamemnon severely (IX, 32–49). The constitution of the Greeks at Troy is of course not democratic, but it is not difficult to trace here the beginnings of the Greek democratic spirit.

In their general manners the heroes observe the rules of orderly and civilised social behaviour. In the ritual of the meal and the sacrifice, there is a regular regard for proprieties. The formulaic character of the verse, in which there is repetition of customary actions, gives a strong impression of an orderly world of shared values and respect for tradition. The heroes habitually address each other with politeness and restraint. Even the gods address favoured mortals in a seemly manner. Priam is treated with exquisite tact by Hermes in disguise (XXIV, 331–447). Women (including Helen) are treated with attention, consideration and respect. In Homer they enjoy more freedom in their relations with men than seems to have been the case in later Greek history. When they discover that they are hereditary guest friends, Glaucus and Diomedes refrain from fighting and exchange gifts (VI, 212–35). Even under the stress of war the civilised decencies of the heroic world are generally maintained.

Excesses in the poem stand out against a background of moderate behaviour. Achilles's refusal to eat before the fight is in marked contrast to the good sense of Odysseus (XIX, 216–37), and also to the advice he himself gives to Priam (XXIV, 559–620). Achilles's abuse of Hector's corpse contrasts with the civilised way in which he treats the dead of Andromache's family. The most obvious barbarities in the *Iliad* stand condemned by standards of civilised behaviour that are the norm in the heroic world.

The anger of Achilles: the tragic pattern

First and foremost the *Iliad* and the *Odyssey* are the definitive epics of Greek literature. They have magnitude and breadth, and depict an heroic world, that is, a world in which heroes and heroic ideals are possible and exist, but in their structure and form, as Aristotle pointed out, the Homeric epics have much in common with Greek tragedy. There is in both Greek epic and Greek tragedy an underlying concentration and unity of design. In the case of the *Odyssey* this is as far as the comparison with tragedy can usefully go. The epic ends happily; Odysseus returns home, is reunited with his wife and restores order in his house. The *Odyssey* has sometimes been called a comedy in the limited sense that it is not tragic. With its 'comedy of Olympus' the *Iliad* too has humorous elements that are in an obvious sense comic, but the comparison with tragedy is obviously more appropriate. In fact Achilles is an archetypal tragic figure and the main plot involving his anger has features regarded by Aristotle as essential for the best sort of tragedy. That is, it contains error (hamartia), reversal (peripeteia), calamity (pathos), and recognition (anagnoresis). Though the precise application of these terms in Aristotle's analysis has been much debated, they have always been useful tools in the discussion of tragedy and together they constitute in a simple form the classic tragic pattern. This pattern, famously described in Aristotle's critical analysis, can first be observed in the *Iliad*.

The initial error occurs in the opening quarrel. Even if we accept Nestor's feeling that there is error on both sides and that Achilles should have submitted quietly to Agamemnon's greater authority (I, 274–84) as Diomedes does later (IV, 401–2), it is clear that Agamemnon is chiefly to blame. In Achilles's eyes Agamemnon abuses his power and is guilty of hubris, arrogant behaviour that offends the gods (I, 203). He prays that Agamemnon will rue his folly in not honouring the best of the Greeks (I, 411–12). The Greek word for folly here is *ate*. It can be used to express an act of folly, the state of being in folly and the consequences of folly. More than folly, it is associated with delusion, blindness and recklessness. The word is personified in Book IX (lines 504–12). Agamemnon is rebuked for bad judgment and stupidity by Thersites (II, 225–42), Odysseus (IV, 349–55), Diomedes (IX, 32–49) and Nestor (IX, 96–113). He admits his own folly (*ate*) privately before the Greek elders (IX, 115–16) and publicly before the army (XIX, 72–144).

The blame for the quarrel between Agamemnon and Achilles falls decisively on Achilles in Book IX when overtures are made to him by the Greek leaders; now his error is greater. Admittedly Agamemnon does not come himself (though no Greek leader suggested he should) and admittedly we know that he still wants Achilles to submit to his authority (IX, 158–61), even though Odysseus does not report this to Achilles, but Agamemnon's gifts (in addition to Briseis) are generous and go beyond what was required by good form alone. The appeal of Odysseus is cunning, referring as it does to the advice of Achilles's father Peleus that he should subdue his haughty spirit (*thumos*) for the sake of friendly feeling (*philophrosune*) (IX, 252–9) and tempting Achilles with the prospect of the honour which the Greeks will bestow on him (IX, 301–3). Achilles replies that the gifts mean nothing to him; he wants nothing less than the humiliation of Agamemnon. The speech of Phoenix that follows makes it clear how far the balance has tipped against Achilles. He who does not show reverence (*aidos*) for the Prayers that seek to undo the harm done by Ate will himself be undone (IX, 496–514). Achilles is now identified as the man of error, folly and delusion. The tale of Meleager offers the heroic precedent of a character who acted too late to be honoured by those he saved (IX, 524–99). Achilles asserts that he has no need of such honour; he is content to have been honoured by Zeus (now that the Greeks are being hard pressed as he had prayed they might be, at I, 408–10). His assertion (IX, 607–8) is reminiscent of the haughty reply given to him by Agamemnon in the opening quarrel (I, 174–5). The blunt speech of Ajax who cannot understand why Achilles is so overwrought makes it clear that by all the normal standards of the heroic society, Achilles should have accepted the gifts since gifts can even expiate a homicide, something much more serious than a quarrel over a girl. Ajax is equally concerned that Achilles has no regard for the obligations of friendship, for he has no quarrel with the other Greeks who have always honoured him (IX, 624–42). Achilles virtually admits that what Ajax has said is fair, but the insult to his honour is overriding (IX, 644–55). When the envoys return to the Greek camp, Diomedes finds Achilles's proud behaviour very much in character (IX, 699–700).

It is clear that any of the other Greek leaders would have yielded, but Achilles is not like any of the other Greeks and this makes him a tragic character. So absolute is his sense of his own worth and honour that he proves inexorable. Like all Homer's characters Achilles is simply drawn. His nature as we see it in the *Iliad* is famously expressed by the Roman poet and critic Horace (65–8BC). If he is to be put upon the stage let him be:

> impiger, iracundus, inexorabilis, acer
> iura neget sibi nata; nihil non arroget armis
> (Art of Poetry, 121–2)

Impatient, quick to anger, ruthless, fierce
Let him say laws are not made for him; let him put
   every question to the sword.

This is largely how we see Achilles in Book IX of the poem.

The response of Achilles to Agamemnon's insult is disproportionate to the offence but it has its origins in something pure and noble. All the heroes share Achilles's heroic aspiration for glory but in none of them is it to be found in so intense a form. In Agamemnon it is tainted with the arrogance of power and the enjoyment of material possession; in Menelaus it is inseparably linked with the desire for revenge and recovery of what is his; in Diomedes it is restrained and moderated; in Odysseus and Nestor it is amenable to tactical and political considerations; in Ajax it is largely unconscious to the extent that occasionally his brute strength is slightly comic; in Paris it is put aside for the sake of pleasure and in Hector it is complicated by the needs of those dependent upon him. Glaucus and Sarpedon fight partly to maintain their position among the Lycians. Only in Achilles is the aspiration pure and simple. He is not greatly interested in the Greek cause; he does not feel he has been wronged by the Trojans (I, 152-60), and he is not fighting for hearth and home like the great patriot Hector who is his opponent. Achilles is bent upon heroic achievement for its own sake not for what it brings with it in the way of material possessions, social position, a just revenge or the defence of loved ones. He fights simply and solely for glory. This purity of motive and aspiration is reflected in the choice he makes in remaining at Troy, preferring a short life with glory to a long life without fame (IX, 410-16). This choice itself is proof of magnanimity of spirit and there is nothing that the magnanimous Achilles would like better than to share his glory with his beloved comrade in arms Patroclus (XVI, 97-100). With this purity of motive Achilles has an absolute sense of his own worth and of the honour due to him because of it. Any diminution of this honour diminishes the whole man for honour is indivisible, and renders his choice of life null and void. There is honourable truth in this feeling, and Achilles honours this single truth so absolutely that he is blind to all other truths, so that his purity proves to be the ruin not only of many others but of himself too. His exceptional sense of personal honour springing from his single-minded and untainted aspiration to glory is at once the source of his greatness and of his great error. This paradox lies at the heart of Homer's tragic vision.

In Book XVI, the pivot of the main action, comes the reversal that results in unforeseen and calamitous consequences. Even Patroclus remarks to the stubborn Achilles that while doctors are treating the leading Greeks, Achilles alone is untreatable (XVI, 21-35). When Achilles relents to the point of allowing Patroclus to fight in his place wearing his armour, there are the first signs of a recognition of his error, as Achilles admits that a man cannot be angry for ever (XVI, 60-1). The concern for his honour is still overriding; Patroclus must only save the ships; he must not fight on to Troy or he will diminish the honour of Achilles (XVI, 80–90). But there is magnanimity as well as irony in his final wish that both he and Patroclus may survive to take Troy together (XVI, 97–100).

The calamitous death of Patroclus, whom he loves more than his own life (XVIII, 81–2), becomes the calamity of Achilles. When the news reaches him, Achilles in conversation with Thetis fully recognises his own error and folly. The gods have done much for him but there is no pleasure in achievement any more. He is ready for death, regrets his special destiny as the son of a goddess and recognises the insidious effects of anger that can darken the wisest mind, is sweeter than honey and spreads like smoke. But the quarrel must be put behind him, and he yields to necessity, accepting the fate which Thetis has revealed to him. Even Heracles, the favourite of Zeus, was finally subdued by the anger of Hera. Achilles resolves to seek glory and the death of Hector (XVIII, 79–126).

In the ensuing fight, Achilles, whose purity of motive is now tainted by the desire for revenge into which his anger has been newly channelled, is resolute for death. His encounter with Aeneas (Book XX) has none of the chivalry that characterised the duels of Paris and Menelaus (Book III), Glaucus and Diomedes (Book VI), or Hector and Ajax (Book VII) in the earlier part of the poem. He captures twelve young Trojans to sacrifice on the pyre of Patroclus (XXI, 27–32, and XXIII, 175–6). He is deaf to the pleas of the suppliant Lycaon whom he had spared on a previous occasion (XXI, 34–135). His arrogant challenge to the river god (XXI, 136–383) contrasts with the restrained war against the gods waged by Diomedes with the support of Athene (Book V). The darkening moral tone of the poem is apparent in the many images of corpses exposed to dogs and carrion birds. In the final combat, the chivalrous Hector proposes a compact whereby the victor does no more than take the spoils of the loser, restoring his body for burial (XXII, 254–9). These are the conditions that had been agreed on in the earlier combat with Ajax (VII, 76–86). Achilles will have none of it: 'Men cannot make compacts with lions' (XXII, 261–72). After the fatal blow, Achilles in a murderous mood tells Hector that dogs and birds of prey will pull him to pieces (XXII, 335–6). With his dying breath Hector again begs for mercy for his corpse (XXII, 338–43). Achilles again refuses in fury; he wishes he could tear him up into pieces and eat him himself, but certainly the dogs and birds will feast upon him (XXII, 345–54). He then fastens Hector's body to his chariot and drags him away. For several days at dawn he hauls Hector's corpse three times around the funeral mound of Patroclus. As she had said farewell to Hector, Andromache recalled how Achilles had chivalrously reverenced the bodies of her family killed at Thebe (VI, 414–28). How far below his previous magnanimity has he now fallen: so far that his behaviour becomes offensive to the gods who put a stop to it (XXIV, 1–92).

The character of Achilles is not good in any other sense than that he excels others in physical prowess and is the best fighter. This physical excellence is the expression of a mighty spirit (*thumos*). But it is a dubious gift that both ennobles and reduces. Homer rarely comments on his characters directly. Either they comment upon each other, as when Helen characterises the leading Greeks to Priam (III, 161–242) or they are characterised indirectly by their words and actions as in the case of Agamemnon, Nestor and Achilles in Book I. But when late in the poem Achilles refuses mercy to one of his opponents in battle, Homer points out the futility of asking mercy from one who is not mild-spirited or of a gentle disposition but is *emmemaos*, impetuous or lost in passion (XX, 467–8). The Greek word here seems to be derived from the verb *mao* meaning to 'strive for', 'to yearn' or 'to desire greatly'. Certainly the passions and aspirations of Achilles like those of other heroes interlock and are inseparable. This close interrelation is emphasised in the tragic pattern of the *Iliad*.

The fall from greatness that is one of the leading ideas of Aristotle in the *Poetics* and is traditionally associated with the tragic protagonist is not so obviously marked in the *Iliad* as, for example, in Sophocles's *King Oedipus* or Shakespeare's *Macbeth*, since the poem opens with the anger which is to distort Achilles's magnanimity. There is no obvious before and after. We have occasional glimpses of Achilles before he was overtaken by anger in the reminiscences of Andromache and Lycaon, but essentially our idea of Achilles's magnanimity comes from the utterances of Achilles himself. Paradoxically we hear of the heroic choice of glory at Troy at the very moment when Achilles is threatening to throw it away by going home (IX, 410–16) so that our idea of Achilles's greatness is inextricably linked with the anger that threatens its overthrow and ruin. This has the effect of enforcing the central tragic paradox that Achilles's greatness and heroism are inextricably bound up with his brutal and ruinous behaviour. In his anger we see the character of the man; this is the kind of person who consciously makes such a stark choice of glory and fame at the expense of a long life, and this is how he behaves when provoked. In the familiar phrase, character is destiny.

In the final book comes the second and fullest recognition scene in the meeting with Priam. Here Achilles is restored to humanity by the pleas of Priam who reminds him of his own aged father Peleus. In his gentle treatment of Priam there is true magnanimity. Achilles looks beyond his own grief and anger, and comes to a calm and steady recognition that men can do no more than bear the indiscriminate mixture of good and bad that comes from Zeus. In the examples of Peleus and Priam he sees the insecurity and incompleteness of human happiness; grief is of little use in the face of the inevitability of human suffering (XXIV, 518–51). In his acceptance and resolution here we find the noble simplicity and quiet grandeur that have often been acknowledged to be the hallmarks of a Classic spirit. How vulnerable and fragile this is before the onset of passion is wonderfully clear in the momentary anger that flares up in Achilles when Priam is impatient to see Hector. But Achilles collects himself, and he urges Priam to share a meal. The taking of food symbolises the practical acceptance of continuing life and the recognition that even the passion of grief must yield to necessity. Amid the ruins of human hope and in the knowledge of imminent death, Achilles for the first time sees life steadily and sees it whole.

A tragic sense of life is distinctively Greek and is implicit in the myths which Homer inherited. The Olympian gods, created in man's image, are imaginative creations that express a sublime belief in human powers and physical beauty. They are created from the consciousness that beauty and excellence in the here and now are the summit of human aspiration. There is no compensating belief in a future reward after death, for Hades is an insubstantial world of twilight consciousness; nor is there in Greek myth a belief in the purposeful working out of the divine will in human history. Troy does not fall because of the righteous anger of Zeus. Zeus himself must submit to fate, even though he would like to save Sarpedon (XVI, 431–61). At the same time the Olympian gods express an acute awareness that man is prey to conflicting amoral forces beyond human control. In this dual consciousness of the potential excellence of human capacities and their vulnerability to capricious and arbitrary powers is the potential for tragedy.

There are three myths in Homer that together illustrate on a small scale the essential features of this dual consciousness. The story of Bellerophon told by Glaucus to Diomedes (VI, 156–205) celebrates heroic excellence. Bellerophon has beauty, magnanimity and physical power. His excellence is tested and not found wanting but even so for no apparent reason he suffers at the hands of the gods, losing a son to Ares and a daughter to Artemis. The story of Meleager told by Phoenix to Achilles (IX, 524–99) shows a hero who uses his strength to save the community in ridding Aetolia of the menace of a wild boar sent by Artemis to terrorise the people because their king had forgotten to offer a sacrifice to her alone of the immortals. In the subsequent war resulting from the struggle for the boar's carcase, he saves the city of Calydon. Thirdly Achilles reminds Priam of the unfortunate Niobe who compared herself to Leto, mother of Apollo and Artemis, and boasted of her larger progeny, thus angering the goddess. Her six sons and six daughters were killed by Apollo and Artemis. They could not be buried because Zeus had turned all the people to stone, until the gods relented after ten days and buried the children themselves. Niobe, now herself turned to stone, broods over the miseries the gods have sent her (XXIV, 602–17). Common to all these stories is pride in human achievement (whether legitimate or presumptuous) and the anger of the gods which, whether deserved or undeserved, is disproportionate to the offence.

In its abbreviated form, the myth of Achilles manifests the dual consciousness apparent in all Greek myths. The myth is first and foremost an heroic myth. Zeus allows Thetis to produce a child who will excel all heroes (XVIII, 436–7). But Thetis tells Achilles that Destiny has given him a choice. If he stays at Troy he can win undying fame, but must himself die there; if he goes back home he can have a long life without glory (IX, 410–16). No reason is given as to why Achilles should have to make this choice; it has the arbitrariness typical of Greek myth. Perhaps there is the idea in the myth that everything has its price, and that the greatest glory exacts the greatest price. But in its pristine form, the myth expresses the heroism of Achilles, who consciously makes an heroic choice in the full knowledge of its ultimate cost. The Homeric Achilles is of course a supreme hero, but Homer has developed the tragic possibilities latent in the myth. The heroic choice is taken for granted and is of secondary significance. The centre of Homer's action is the defeat of heroic expectation through folly and passion. Achilles is not a hero in control of his destiny but the victim of the arbitrary power of another man's folly and the imperious demands of his own nature. What happens to him in the poem is determined not by any external decree of the gods but by his own absolute sense of his personal honour. The climax of the poem is not the full-hearted celebration of heroic achievement but an act in which the glory of the hero is clearly tarnished. The knowledge in which the greater humanity of the hero is revealed is not the confident knowledge of what his own heroic choice has cost him, but a bitter recognition of his own error and then an acceptance of necessary suffering as the universal condition, which quite transcends the original heroic myth. The tragic pattern imposed by Homer upon the heroic myth reveals a depth of humanity beyond the heroism of the hero.

The Greek view of the world as reflected in the myths is given a fully tragic form in the *Iliad*, through the development in the main action of the tragic pattern arising from the anger of Achilles. In this development and in the experience of Achilles lies the main burden of the poem's meaning. The pattern of the main action is simple and clear; its tragic effect is achieved through careful organisation and through the intensity with which it is expressed and made real.

Part 4

Hints for study

Some Homeric questions and problems

The following are a few of the many questions and problems that have been raised by readers of the *Iliad* over the centuries. Not all of them are equally justified or sensible, but there is profit to be gained from determining the grounds upon which a particular question may be inappropriate.

1. Apollo and Athene take part in the action of Book I. Thetis later tells Achilles that all the gods are away feasting in Ethiopia for twelve days. What is to be made of this inconsistency?

2. What is the point of Agamemnon's test of the army (II, 73)? Is it adequately motivated?

3. Why should Priam need to be told about the Greek leaders in the tenth year of the siege of Troy (III, 161–242)?

4. In the council on Olympus (IV, 1–72), why is no reference made to Zeus's promise to Thetis?

5. Pylaemenes killed at V, 576 is alive at XIII, 658. What conclusion can be drawn from this inconsistency?

6. 'If you are a god, I am not the sort to fight against the immortals', says Diomedes (VI, 128–9) to the unknown Glaucus, having just wounded Aphrodite and Ares (in Book V). What is to be made of this apparent inconsistency?

7. In the exchange between Hector and Paris (VI, 313–41) no mention is made of the latter's recent duel with Menelaus (Book III). Is this not puzzling?

8. Why should the Greeks agree to a second duel (VII, 91–102) after the Trojans have broken their oaths in the first?

9. Why should it suddenly occur to the Greeks in the tenth year of the siege to build a defensive wall to protect their ships at a time when they are winning?

10. Is the inexorability of Achilles in Book IX consistent with his later attitudes (in Books XI and XVI)?

11. Why is Phoenix, Achilles's old retainer, with Agamemnon and not with Achilles (IX, 168)?

12. Are the actions of Diomedes and Odysseus in Book X consistent with the standards of behaviour that are shown in the rest of the poem as the accepted norm in the heroic world?

13. Does Nestor's long account of his youthful prowess (XI, 656–762) serve any useful purpose in its context?
14. Poseidon has been helping the Greeks quite successfully in Book XIII. Is the deception of Zeus in Book XIV a) necessary, or b) should it have come earlier?
15. How successfully does Homer keep the reader's interest during the fighting in the middle section of the poem (Books XII–XV)?
16. 'Attend while I tell you what to do so that all the Greeks may honour me and restore the lovely girl and give splendid gifts' (XVI, 83–6). How do these words of Achilles to Patroclus stand in relation to the embassy to Achilles in Book IX?
17. Why does Homer delay (until Book XVIII) the bringing of the news of Patroclus's death to Achilles?
18. After the magnificent return of Achilles to the fighting, is not the encounter with Aeneas (XX, 79–352) with its long conversation and lack of vigorous action an anticlimax?
19. Is the battle of the gods (XX, 385–513) consistent with the dignity of epic?
20. Would the poem be better without the last two books, thus ending with the climactic action of the death of Hector?

Use of the critical heritage and translation

Again, with respect to . . . the classical writers of antiquity: . . . all I say is, let us study them. They can help to cure us of what is, it seems to me, the great vice of our intellect, manifesting itself in our incredible vagaries in literature, in art, in religion, in morals: namely that it is *fantastic*, and wants *sanity*. Sanity – that is the great virtue of the ancient literature; the want of that is the great defect of the modern, in spite of all its variety and power. It is impossible to read carefully the great ancients, without losing something of our caprice and eccentricity.

(Matthew Arnold (1822–88), the Victorian critic and poet, in 'Preface to Poems' (1854)

Because the Homeric poems exist in an historical vacuum, the student of Homer cannot deepen his knowledge and appreciation of the original by relating the poems to their contemporary context. Nor is there much to be gained from reading the vast literature upon the Homeric question. Of much greater value to the student of Homer is knowledge of what Homer has meant to subsequent poets, critics and translators. To discover what men of great creative imagination have thought and felt about Homer cannot fail to result in a heightened awareness of the quality of the poetry. For the reader with no Greek, in particular, the study of translations is hardly just an academic exercise; to read Homer in prose or in a dull verse translation is like reading Shakespeare in modern English. To overcome this requires an imaginative effort on the part of the student and diligent use of the few good poetic versions available.

What follows here is a short anthology of comments and translations which is meant both to throw further light upon Homer and to suggest the ways in which students can benefit in their own study by the judicious use of translations and critical comments. The extracts are given not in strict chronological order of their publication, but rather by affinity of theme or treatment.

Mention has already been made of Aristotle's famous remarks on the form of Homeric epic. Of particular value in Classical literature is the appreciation of Homer contained in the treatise *On the Sublime* attributed to the Greek critic Longinus and probably written sometime in the first century AD. For Longinus Homer is pre-eminently a poet who writes in the grand style. He quotes many passages from the *Iliad* to illustrate Homeric grandeur, usually in connection with the gods, quoting, for example, the moment when Hera's horses leap majestically from Olympus to Troy. Here it is in the version of the eighteenth-century poet and translator of Homer, Alexander Pope (1688–1744):

> Far as a shepherd from some point on high
> O'er the wide main extends his boundless eye
> Through such a space of air, with thund'ring sound
> At ev'ry leap the immortal coursers* bound
>
> *Iliad*, V, 770–2/Pope, *ll.* 959–62

But by sublimity Longinus does not merely mean grandeur. He defines the true sublime as any literary passage that has the power to elevate the reader and take him out of himself. The truly beautiful and sublime is what can be seen to have this effect on diverse people in different times (*On the Sublime*, VII).

One such passage that has been much admired is the moment when Hector takes his farewell of Andromache in Book VI. Here it is in the version of the great poet and translator of the seventeenth century, John Dryden (1631–1700) in *The Last Parting of Hector and Andromache* (1693):

> He said –
> Then, holding forth his arms, he took his boy
> (The pledge of love and other hope of Troy).
> The fearful infant turn'd his head away,
> And on his nurse's neck reclining lay,

*coursers: horses

His unknown father shunning with affright,
And looking back on so uncouth a sight;
Daunted to see a face with steel o'erspread,
And his high plume that nodded o'er his head.
His sire and mother smil'd with silent joy,
And Hector hasten'd to relieve his boy;
Dismissed his burnish'd helm, that shone afar
(The pride of warriors, and the pomp of war):
Th' illustrious babe, thus reconcil'd, he took;
Hugg'd in his arms, and kiss'd, and thus he spoke:
'Parent of gods and men, propitious Jove
And you bright synod of the pow'rs above;
On this my son your gracious gifts bestow;
Grant him to live, and great in arms to grow;
To reign in Troy, to govern with renown,
To shield the people, and assert the crown:
That, when hereafter he from war shall come
And bring his Trojans peace and triumph home,
Some aged man, who lives this act to see,
And who in former times remember'd me,
May say the son in fortitude and fame
Out-goes the mark, and drowns his father's name:
That at these words his mother may rejoice,
And add her suffrage to the public voice.'
                              Thus having said,
He first with suppliant hands the gods ador'd:
Then to the mother's arms the child restor'd:
With tears and smiles she took her son, and press'd
The illustrious infant to her fragrant breast.
                    Iliad, VI, 466–84/Dryden, *ll*. 141–74

Pope appended the following note to his own version of this passage in Homer:

There never was a finer piece of painting than this. Hector extends his arms to embrace his child; the child affrighted at the glittering of his helmet and the shaking of the plume, shrinks backward to the breast of his nurse; Hector unbraces his helmet, lays it on the ground, takes the infant in his arms, lifts him towards heaven, and offers a prayer for him to the gods: then returns him to the mother Andromache who receives him with a smile of pleasure, but at the same instant the fears of her husband make her burst into tears. All these are but small circumstances, but so artfully chosen, that every reader immediately feels the force of them, and represents the whole in the utmost liveliness to his imagination. This alone might be a confutation of that false criticism some have fallen into, who affirm that a poet ought only to collect the great and noble particulars in his paintings. But it is in the images of things as in the characters of persons; where a small action, or even a small circumstance of an action, lets us more into the knowledge and comprehension of them, than the material and principal parts themselves . . . . There is a vast difference betwixt a small circumstance and a trivial one, and the smallest become important if they are well chosen, and not confused.

Homer's narrative style includes so much. There is the grandeur of Hector's prayer for a heroic future for his child, which is full of pathos and irony because of Hector's foreboding and the reader's knowledge that Troy will fall. But into this scene of great pathos and grandeur enters the human reality of the small child's fear of the nodding plume which causes laughter amidst the tears and makes the moment of parting one of tender intimacy so that heroism is given a fully human context. This simple and direct portrayal of human nature, unhampered by any distracting notion of false grandeur, is what Homer has been admired for throughout the ages. 'His positions are natural and his representations are general with very little dependence upon local or temporary customs', wrote the English critic Dr Johnson (1709–84).* Homer's grand style is not therefore an exclusive one; there is nothing solemn about it; it includes the familiar touch, descends to particular details of common human experience and can tolerate the intrusion of the comic. Itself comprehensive, it expresses a comprehensive view of life.

In his lectures *On Translating Homer* (1861), Matthew Arnold offered his famous identification of four characteristic features of Homer's style and commented upon the difficulty which they presented to translators:

the translator of Homer should above all be penetrated by a sense of four qualities of his author: – that he is eminently rapid; that he is eminently plain and direct, both in the evolution of his thought and the expression of it, that is, both in his syntax and in his words; that he is eminently plain and direct in the substance of his thought, that is, in his matter and ideas . . . . And yet, in spite of this perfect plainness and directness of his ideas, he is eminently *noble*; he works as entirely in the grand style, he is as grandiose, as Phidias [the most famous ancient sculptor of the fourth century BC] or Dante [the great medieval Italian poet (1265–1321) and author of the *Divine*

*See his comments on Pope's Homer in his 'Life of Pope' in Samuel Johnson, *Lives of the English Poets*, ed. L. Archer-Hind, Everyman's Library, Dent, London, 1964, II, pp. 157–73 and 223–4.

Comedy] or Michael Angelo [the great Renaissance painter and sculptor (1475–1564)]. This is what makes his translators despair. 'To give relief' says Cowper [William Cowper (1731–1800) who translated Homer in the late eighteenth century] 'to prosaic subjects' (such as dressing, eating, drinking, harnessing, travelling, going to bed), that is to treat such subjects nobly, in the grand style, 'without seeming unseasonably tumid, is extremely difficult'. It *is* difficult, but Homer has done it. Homer is precisely the incomparable poet he is, because he has done it. His translation must not be tumid, must not be artificial, must not be literary; true; but then also he must not be commonplace, must not be ignoble.

For Arnold, as for Longinus, Homer is pre-eminently a poet who writes in the grand style. The sublimity of Homer's Classic style affords the rare pleasure of the highest art, an experience radically different from that afforded by contemporary Victorian translations in the ballad manner.

Given the difficulties inherent in translation, success in representing the original can only be partial. Logic and common sense require us to accept that the uniqueness of a work of art cannot really be translated at all. But a creative writer inspired by the genius of the original may reproduce for his own age and in his own language a version that translates essential features, even if it must fail to recapture the whole. What do we require of a successful translation of Homer? For Alexander Pope, writing in the preface to his own translation of 1720, Homer's leading characteristic is his power of animation:

> It is to the strength of this amazing invention we are to attribute that unequalled fire and rapture which is so forcible in Homer, that no man of a true poetical spirit is master of himself while he reads him. What he writes is of the most animated nature imaginable; everything moves, everything lives, and is put in action . . . . That which, in my opinion, ought to be the endeavour of any one who translates Homer, is above all things to keep alive that spirit and fire which makes his chief character.

The most fiery and spirited version of Homer is the translation of Book I made by John Dryden and published in his *Fables* of 1700. It is necessary to read it entire, but two extracts may suggest its quality. The first shows the vigorous passion with which Dryden renders the anger of Achilles:

> At her departure his disdain return'd:
> The fire she fann'd with greater fury burn'd;
> Rumbling within, till thus it found a vent:
> 'Dastard and drunkard, mean and insolent;

Tongue-valiant hero, vaunter of thy might,
In threats the foremost, but the lag* in fight;
When didst thou thrust amid the mingled prease†
Content to bide the war aloof in peace?
Arms are the trade of each plebeian soul;
'Tis death to fight, but kingly to control;
Lord-like at ease with arbitrary power,
To peel‡ the chiefs, the people to devour.
These, traitor, are thy talents, safer far
Than to contend in fields, and toils of war.
Nor couldst thou thus have dar'd the common hate,
Were not their souls as abject as their state.
But, by this scepter, solemnly I swear
(Which never more green leaf or growing branch shall bear;
Torn from the tree and given by Jove to those
Who laws dispense, and mighty wrongs oppose)
That when the Grecians want my wonted aid,
No gift shall bribe it and no prayer persuade.
When Hector comes, the homicide, to wield
His conquering arms, with corps to show the field;
Then shalt thou mourn thy pride, and late confess
My wrong repented when 'tis past redress.'
He said; and with disdain in open view,
Against the ground his golden scepter threw
                    Iliad, I, 233–46/Dryden, *ll.* 332–59

The fiery spirit that flares up in the quarrel between Achilles and Agamemnon is felt, too, in a transmogrified form in the quarrel on Olympus between Zeus and Hera (whom Dryden calls by their Roman names Jupiter or Jove and Juno).

He moves into his hall: the powers resort,
Each from his house, to fill the sovereign's court.
Nor waiting summons, nor expecting stood;
But met with reverence, and received the god.
He mounts the throne; and Juno took her place;
But sullen discontent sat low'ring on her face.
With jealous eyes, at distance she had seen,
Whispering with Jove, the silver-footed queen;
Then impotent of tongue (her silence broke),
Thus turbulent in rattling tone she spoke:
'Author of ills, and close contriver Jove,
Which of thy dames, what prostitute of love,

---

*lag: slow or reluctant to fight   †prease: press, crowd of fighting men   ‡peel: strip

Has held thy ear so long, and begg'd so hard,
For some old service done, some new reward?
Apart you talk'd, for that's your special care;
The consort never must the council share.
One gracious word is for a wife too much:
Such is a marriage vow, and Jove's own faith is such.' . . .
To whom the Thunderer made this stern reply:
'My household curse, my lawful plague, the spy
Of Jove's designs, his other squinting eye;
Why this vain prying, and for what avail?
Jove will be master still and Juno fail.
Should they suspicious thoughts divine aright
Thou but becom'st more odious to my sight
For this attempt: uneasy life for me,
Still watch'd and importun'd, but worse for thee.
Curb that impetuous tongue, before too late
The gods behold, and tremble at thy fate
Pitying, but daring not, in thy defense,
To lift a hand against omnipotence.'
    This heard, the imperious queen sat mute with fear,
Nor further durst incense the gloomy Thunderer.
Iliad, I, 533–43; 560–9/Dryden, *ll.* 715–32; 751–65

Here the dignified and elegant style of Dryden can accommodate comedy, but the effect is controlled and far from being burlesque. Jupiter may be a henpecked husband but he remains a formidable and powerful god.

While the version of George Chapman (?1559–?1634) does not have the finished artistry of the later neoclassical versions of Dryden and Pope, his *Iliad* of 1616 does have great spirit and vigour. His translation of the following simile typifies his response to the physical energy of the original:

              – And as a huge ox hide
A Currier* gives amongst his men to supple and extend
With oil, till it be drunk withall; they tug, stretch out and spend
Their oil and liquor liberally, and chafe the leather so
That out they make a vapour breathe, and in their oil doth go;
A number of them set on work, and in an orb they pull
That all ways all parts of the hide they may extend at full:
So here and there did both parts hale† the corse‡ in little place
And wrought it all ways with their sweat.
                Iliad, XVII, 389–95/Chapman, *ll.* 335–41

*Currier: one who dresses leather after it is tanned   †hale: pull   ‡corse: corpse

Here is Achilles's ruthless reply to Hector in the final combat:

'Hector, thou only pestilence in all mortality
To my sere spirits, never set the point twixt thee and me
Any conditions: but as far as men and lions fly
All terms of covenant, lambs and wolves, in so far opposite state
(Impossible for love t'atone) stand we, till our souls satiate
The god of soldiers. Do not dream that our disjunction can
Endure condition. Therefore now all worth that fits a man
Call to thee, all particular parts that fit a soldier;
And they all this include (besides the skill and spirit of war)
Hunger for slaughter, and a hate that eats thy heart to eat
Thy foe's heart. This stirs, this supplies in death the killing heat;
And all this needst thou. No more flight. Pallas Athenia
Will quickly cast thee to my lance. Now, now together drawn
All griefs for vengeance, both in me and all my friends late dead
That bled thee, raging with thy lance.'

Iliad, XXII, 261–72/Chapman, *ll.* 224–38

Gone are the simplicity, the directness and the clarity of Homer, but there is a creative response here to the underlying realities of the original.

Pope's version of 1720 is vigorous and clear, and should be read in conjunction with the notes he published with it. Here is his translation of a famous moment in which the ruthless Achilles denies Lycaon's plea for mercy:

'Talk not of life, or ransom (he replies)
Patroclus dead, whoever meets me, dies:
In vain a single Trojan sues for grace;
But least, the sons of Priam's hateful race.
Die then, my friend! what boots it* to deplore?
The great, the good Patroclus is no more!
He, far thy better, was foredoom'd to die,
And thou, dost thou bewail mortality?
Seest thou not me, whom nature's gifts adorn,
Sprung from a hero, from a goddess born?
The day shall come (which nothing can avert)
When by the spear, the arrow, or the dart,
By night, or day, by force, or by design,
Impending death and certain fate are mine!
Die then,' – He said, and as the word he spoke,
The fainting stripling sank before the stroke.

Iliad, XXI, 99–114/Pope, *ll.* 111–26

---

*what boots it: what use is it

Pope commented on this speech: 'There is an air of greatness in the conclusion of the speech of Achilles, which strikes me very much: He speaks very unconcernedly of his own death, and upbraids his enemy for asking life so earnestly, a life that was of so much less importance than his own.'

Pope's narrative is rapid, always elevated, and sensitive to dramatic climax:

> Swift was the course; no vulgar prize they play,
> No vulgar victim must reward the day,
> (Such as in races crown the speedy strife)
> The prize contended was great Hector's life.
>
> *Iliad*, XXII, 159–61/Pope, *ll.* 207–10

He is particularly good at moments of general moral reflection as when Apollo withdraws from the fighting with the following observation:

> For what is man? Calamitous by birth
> They owe their life and nourishment to earth;
> Like yearly leaves, that now, with beauty crown'd
> Smile on the sun; now, wither on the ground.
>
> *Iliad*, XXI, 463–6/Pope, *ll.* 537–40

Pope comments: 'The poet is very happy in interspersing his poem with moral sentences; in this place he steals away his reader from war and horror, and gives him a beautiful admonition of his own frailty.'

Here is the noble admonition of Achilles to Priam:

> Rise then: let reason mitigate our care:
> To mourn avails not: man is born to bear.
> Such is, alas! the gods' severe decree
> They, only they are blest, and only free . . . .
> What must be, must be. Bear thy lot, nor shed
> These unavailing sorrows o'er the dead;
> Thou can'st not call him from the Stygian shore
> But thou alas! may'st live, to suffer more!
>
> *Iliad*, XXIV, 522–6; 549–51/Pope, *ll.* 599–62; 692–5

Pope comments:

> There is not a more beautiful passage in the whole *Iliad* than this before us: Homer to show that Achilles was not a mere soldier, here draws him as a person of excellent sense and sound reason . . . . And it was a piece of great judgement thus to describe him; for the reader would have retained but a very indifferent opinion of the hero of a poem, that had no qualification but mere strength: It also shows the art of the poet thus to defer this part of his character till the very

conclusion of the poem: By these means he fixes an idea of his greatness upon our minds, and makes his hero go off the stage with applause.

There is pathos, and tender feeling, in his translation, apparent in his version of Helen's lament for Hector:

Ah dearest friend! in whom the gods had join'd
The mildest manners with the bravest mind!
Now twice ten years (unhappy years) are o'er
Since Paris brought me to the Trojan shore;
(Oh had I perish'd, e'er that form divine
Seduc'd this soft, this easy heart of mine!)
Yet was it ne'er my fate, from thee to find
A deed ungentle, or a word unkind:
When others curst the auth'ress of their woe,
Thy pity check'd my sorrows in their flow:
If some proud brother eyed me with disdain,
Or scornful sister with her sweeping train,
Thy gentle accents soften'd all my pain.
For thee I mourn: and mourn my self in thee,
The wretched source of all this misery!
The fate I caus'd, for ever I bemoan;
Sad Helen has no friend now thou art gone!
Thro' Troy's wide streets abandon'd shall I roam,
In Troy deserted, as abhorr'd at home!

Iliad, XXIV, 762–75/Pope, *ll.* 962–80

Introducing this same speech in Homer the nephew of the romantic poet and critic Samuel Coleridge (1722–1834) commented:

Few things are more interesting to observe than how the same hand that has given us the fury and inconsistency of Achilles, gives us also the consummate elegance and tenderness of Helen. She is through the *Iliad* a genuine lady, graceful in motion and speech, noble in her associations, full of remorse for a fault for which higher powers seem responsible, yet grateful and affectionate towards those with whom that fault had committed her. I have always thought the following speech . . . as almost the sweetest passage in the poem.*

Finally, Pope brings to the close of his translation a calm majesty and noble harmony:

Soon as Aurora, daughter of the dawn,
With rosy lustre streak'd the dewy lawn,

*Henry Nelson Coleridge, *Introduction to the Study of the Greek Classic Poets*, John Murray, London, 1830, p. 198.

Again the mournful crowds surround the pyre,
And quench with wine the yet remaining fire.
The snowy bones his friends and brothers place
(With tears collected) in a golden vase;
The golden vase in purple palls they roll'd,
Of softest texture, and inwrought with gold.
Last o'er the urn the sacred earth they spread,
And raised the tomb, memorial of the dead.
(Strong guards and spies, till all the rites were done,
Watch'd from the rising to the setting sun.)
All Troy then moves to Priam's court again,
A solemn, silent, melancholy train:
Assembled there, from pious toil they rest,
And sadly shared the last sepulchral feast.
Such honours Ilion to her hero paid,
And peaceful slept the mighty Hector's shade.

Iliad, XXIV, 788–804/Pope, *ll.* 999–1016

At the end of his own translation of the *Iliad* (1791) William Cowper wrote:

> I cannot take leave of this noble poem without expressing how much I am struck with this plain conclusion of it. It is like the exit of a great man out of company whom he has entertained magnificently; neither pompous, nor familiar; not contemptuous; yet without much ceremony. I recollect nothing, among the works of mere man, that exemplifies so strongly the true style of great antiquity.

Specimen essay

Discuss Homer's art of representation in the making and decoration of the Shield of Achilles.

Hephaestus, the divine artificer, begins by representing on the shield the earth, the sea, the sun, the moon and the constellations. He ends by putting the ocean around the rim of the shield. In Homer the ocean surrounds the earth, so that on the shield is shown a representation of the whole of creation. The scenes depicted upon the shield are from ordinary life not from heroic legend. Together with the images of ordinary peacetime activity in many of the similes, they present an eternal world of human activity transcending the Trojan War.

The god creates two beautiful cities. The first is a city at peace in which weddings are celebrated with music, feasting and dancing. In the market assembly of the people two litigants disputing claims of compensation for a homicide put their case before a tribunal of elders who give judgment and expound the law. In contrast to this picture of peaceful activity and the rule of law is the second city which is in a state of siege. There is an ambush and a bloody battle. Five agricultural scenes follow: the ploughing of a field with a drink of mellow wine for the ploughman; the harvest on the king's estate with a feast for the labourers; the grape-picking by young men and women to the accompaniment of music, song and dancing; the herding of cattle with the intrusion of a lion who carries off a bellowing bull; and lastly the grazing ground for sheep. The final picture is of young men and women dancing to music and delighting a crowd of onlookers.

Though many of the scenes are idyllic the overall representation is not idealised in the sense that men are presented as better than they are. Even in the first city at peace, a homicide has been committed. In the second city the soldiers engage in battle, fight and drag off their dead like real living men (XVIII, 539). It is apparent that what the poet admires most is the realism of the picture and the ability of the god to bring it all to life. The city at war has beauty of its own, justifying Homer's description of both cities as beautiful (XVIII, 491).

There are several touches that testify to the craftsmanship of the god. In the city at war the gods are larger than life and wrought in gold. In the picture of the ploughing the unploughed field is made of gold; behind the plough the colour of the soil is black as in real life, a marvel to behold (XVIII, 549). The vineyard is gold, the grapes are black, the ditches are blue and the fences tin. The cows are of gold and tin. The poet appreciates the divine craftsmanship whereby the god makes the most of his various materials to ensure that vital details stand out in relief.

Homer gives us a vivid impression of the shield's manufacture as the god vigorously sets about his task. The divine craftsmanship of the plastic artist finds its counterpart in the poetic energy with which Homer invests his descriptions of the scenes on the shield. In these there is so much activity and movement that rationalistic critics have been offended because the descriptions no longer accurately represent what is a static object. But Homer is not interested in accurate representation, in verisimilitude, but in lively representation. The art of Homer is not to give us finished pictures but pictures in the making. Homeric art is not still, like a Grecian urn, but always moving and full of energy.

Homer's celebration of the craftsman and the power of his art culminates in the final picture on the shield, the dancing on a beautiful dance floor likened to the famous one built at Cnossus by Daedalus, the legendary Cretan artist and craftsman. The name Daedalus is derived from the Greek word *daidallein*, to embellish or decorate with cunning craftsmanship. The word is used of Hephaestus himself as he begins his task (XVIII, 479), and what the god puts upon the shield is described as many *daidala*, many things cunningly wrought (XVIII, 482).

It is a fine stroke of art on Homer's part that his last picture should celebrate the artist and the dance. Hephaestus begins with a joyful celebration of weddings with music, singing and dancing. He ends with a picture that celebrates youth and movement in the delight of the dance. Though not of noble birth (the girls are dairymaids), the dancers are beautifully dressed. Their dancing is formal in that there is a pattern of movement which involves all of them together, yet it is also energetic. Their movement is compared to the wheel of a potter. The immediate point of the comparison is speed, but the figure also suggests the perfect symmetry of the circle and the regular movement that results in a finished work of art. A great crowd gathers delighting in the spectacle of the dance and the bard sings to the accompaniment of his lyre, yet the final image is again one of energetic movement, but movement not without order. In the midst of the dancers acrobats perform in time to the music.

The dance has both order and energy, formality and spontaneity. In the whole scene the dominant impression is one of a joyous celebration of physical energy. The crowd are charmed by the dance that brings delight (XVIII, 603). But the dance is organised energy, so that the passage also celebrates the power of art, apparent in the underlying pattern of the dance, the mention of Daedalus, the image of the potter's wheel and the presence of the bard and his music. In the Homeric dance the formality of art does not obtrude. Because of this, the dance which celebrates both art and life together is the perfect image with which to conclude the description of the shield.

Part 5

Suggestions for further reading

The text and translations

HOMER: *Opera*, edited by D. B. Monroe, Oxford Classical Texts, Clarendon Press, Oxford, 1906. Includes the *Iliad* and the *Odyssey*.

HOMER: *Iliad*, edited by T. W. Allen, 3 vols, Oxford Classical Texts, Clarendon Press, Oxford, 1931.

HOMER: *Iliad*, edited with an introduction and notes by D. B. Monroe, 2 vols, Clarendon Press Series, 5th edition, revised, Clarendon Press, Oxford, 1899.

HOMER: *The Iliad with an English Translation* by A. T. Murray, Loeb Classical Library, 2 vols, Heinemann, London, Harvard University Press, Cambridge, Mass., 1924.

HOMER: *The Odyssey with an English Translation* by A. T. Murray, Loeb Classical Library, 2 vols, Heinemann, London, Harvard University Press, Cambridge, Mass., 1919.

HOMER: *The Iliad*, trans. E. V. Rieu, Penguin, Harmondsworth, 1950.

HOMER: *The Odyssey*, trans. E. V. Rieu, Penguin, Harmondsworth, 1946.

CHAPMAN, GEORGE: *Chapman's Homer*, edited by Allardyce Nicoll, Volume One, *The Iliad*, Routledge and Kegan Paul, London, 1957.

COWPER, WILLIAM: *The Poetical Works of William Cowper*, edited by H. F. Cary, London, 1855. Contains his *Iliad*.

DRYDEN, JOHN: *The Poetical Works of John Dryden*, edited by James Kinsley, 4 vols, Clarendon Press, Oxford, 1958. 'The Last Parting of Hector and Andromache. From the Sixth Book of Homer's Iliads' in Vol. II, pp. 846–51; 'The First Book of Homer's Iliads' in Vol. IV, pp. 1583–604.

POPE, ALEXANDER: *Translations of Homer. The Iliad*, edited by Maynard Mack (Vols. VII and VIII of *The Twickenham Edition of the Poems of Alexander Pope*, general editor, John Butt), Methuen, London; Yale University Press, New Haven, 1967. This edition reprints his notes.

Works of general reference

Atlas of Ancient and Classical Geography, Everyman's Library, J. M. Dent, London, 1950.

A Companion to Homer, edited by A. J. B. Wace, and F. H. Stubbings, Macmillan, London, 1962.

A Dictionary of Greek and Roman Biography and Mythology, edited by W. Smith, 3 vols, London, 1876.

LEAF, WALTER: *A Companion to the Iliad for English Readers*, Macmillan, London, 1892.

The Oxford Classical Dictionary, edited by N. G. L. Hammond and H. H. Scullard, 2nd edition, Clarendon Press, Oxford, 1970.

SCHERER, M. R.: *The Legends of Troy in Art and Literature*, Phaidon Press, London and New York, 1963.

Criticism of Homer

ARISTOTLE: *Aristotle's Theory of Poetry and Fine Art*, translated with critical notes by S. H. Butcher, 3rd edition, Edinburgh, 1902.

ARNOLD, MATTHEW: *Matthew Arnold: On the Classical Tradition*, edited by R. H. Super, University of Michigan Press, Ann Arbor, 1960. Contains his lectures 'On Translating Homer'.

JOHNSON, SAMUEL: 'The Life of Pope' in *Lives of the English Poets*, edited by L. Archer-Hind, Everyman's Library, 2 vols, J. M. Dent, London, 1964.

'LONGINUS': *Aristotle: The Poetics, 'Longinus': On the Sublime, Demetrius: On Style*, Loeb Classical Library, Heinemann, London, Harvard University Press, Cambridge, Mass., 1932.

MASON, H. A.: *To Homer Through Pope: An Introduction to Homer's Iliad and Pope's Translation*, Chatto and Windus, London, 1972.

OWEN, E. T.: *The Story of the Iliad*, G. Bell & Sons, London, 1947.

The author of these notes

ROBIN SOWERBY was educated at St Catharine's College, Cambridge, where he read Classics and English. Since 1972 he has been a lecturer in the Department of English Studies at Stirling University. He is also the author of York Notes on *The Aeneid*.

York Notes: list of titles

MRS GASKELL
North and South

WILLIAM GOLDING
Lord of the Flies
The Spire

OLIVER GOLDSMITH
She Stoops to Conquer
The Vicar of Wakefield

ROBERT GRAVES
Goodbye to All That

GRAHAM GREENE
Brighton Rock
The Heart of the Matter
The Power and the Glory

WILLIS HALL
The Long and the Short and the Tall

THOMAS HARDY
Far from the Madding Crowd
Jude the Obscure
Selected Poems
Tess of the D'Urbervilles
The Mayor of Casterbridge
The Return of the Native
The Trumpet Major
The Woodlanders
Under the Greenwood Tree

L. P. HARTLEY
The Go-Between
The Shrimp and the Anemone

NATHANIEL HAWTHORNE
The Scarlet Letter

SEAMUS HEANEY
Selected Poems

JOSEPH HELLER
Catch-22

ERNEST HEMINGWAY
A Farewell to Arms
For Whom the Bell Tolls
The Old Man and the Sea

HERMANN HESSE
Steppenwolf

BARRY HINES
Kes

HOMER
The Iliad
The Odyssey

ANTHONY HOPE
The Prisoner of Zenda

GERARD MANLEY HOPKINS
Selected Poems

RICHARD HUGHES
A High Wind in Jamaica

TED HUGHES
Selected Poems

THOMAS HUGHES
Tom Brown's Schooldays

ALDOUS HUXLEY
Brave New World

HENRIK IBSEN
A Doll's House
Ghosts

HENRY JAMES
The Ambassadors
The Portrait of a Lady
Washington Square

SAMUEL JOHNSON
Rasselas

BEN JONSON
The Alchemist
Volpone

JAMES JOYCE
A Portrait of the Artist as a Young Man
Dubliners

JOHN KEATS
Selected Poems

PHILIP LARKIN
Selected Poems

D. H. LAWRENCE
Selected Short Stories
Sons and Lovers
The Rainbow
Women in Love

CAMARA LAYE
L'Enfant Noir

HARPER LEE
To Kill a Mocking-Bird

LAURIE LEE
Cider with Rosie

THOMAS MANN
Tonio Kröger

CHRISTOPHER MARLOWE
Doctor Faustus

ANDREW MARVELL
Selected Poems

W. SOMERSET MAUGHAM
Selected Short Stories

GAVIN MAXWELL
Ring of Bright Water

J. MEADE FALKNER
Moonfleet

HERMAN MELVILLE
Moby Dick

THOMAS MIDDLETON
Women Beware Women

THOMAS MIDDLETON and WILLIAM ROWLEY
The Changeling

ARTHUR MILLER
A View from the Bridge
Death of a Salesman
The Crucible

JOHN MILTON
Paradise Lost I & II
Paradise Lost IV & IX
Selected Poems

V. S. NAIPAUL
A House for Mr Biswas

ROBERT O'BRIEN
Z for Zachariah

SEAN O'CASEY
Juno and the Paycock

GABRIEL OKARA
The Voice

EUGENE O'NEILL
Mourning Becomes Electra

GEORGE ORWELL
Animal Farm
Nineteen Eighty-four

JOHN OSBORNE
Look Back in Anger

WILFRED OWEN
Selected Poems

ALAN PATON
Cry, The Beloved Country

THOMAS LOVE PEACOCK
Nightmare Abbey and *Crotchet Castle*

HAROLD PINTER
The Caretaker

SYLVIA PLATH
Selected Works

PLATO
The Republic

ALEXANDER POPE
Selected Poems

J. B. PRIESTLEY
  An Inspector Calls
THOMAS PYNCHON
  The Crying of Lot 49
SIR WALTER SCOTT
  Ivanhoe
  Quentin Durward
  The Heart of Midlothian
  Waverley
PETER SHAFFER
  The Royal Hunt of the Sun
WILLIAM SHAKESPEARE
  A Midsummer Night's Dream
  Antony and Cleopatra
  As You Like It
  Coriolanus
  Cymbeline
  Hamlet
  Henry IV Part I
  Henry IV Part II
  Henry V
  Julius Caesar
  King Lear
  Love's Labour's Lost
  Macbeth
  Measure for Measure
  Much Ado About Nothing
  Othello
  Richard II
  Richard III
  Romeo and Juliet
  Sonnets
  The Merchant of Venice
  The Taming of the Shrew
  The Tempest
  The Winter's Tale
  Troilus and Cressida
  Twelfth Night
GEORGE BERNARD SHAW
  Androcles and the Lion
  Arms and the Man
  Caesar and Cleopatra
  Candida
  Major Barbara
  Pygmalion
  Saint Joan
  The Devil's Disciple
MARY SHELLEY
  Frankenstein
PERCY BYSSHE SHELLEY
  Selected Poems
RICHARD BRINSLEY SHERIDAN
  The School for Scandal
  The Rivals
R. C. SHERRIFF
  Journey's End
WOLE SOYINKA
  The Road
EDMUND SPENSER
  The Faerie Queene (Book I)
JOHN STEINBECK
  Of Mice and Men
  The Grapes of Wrath
  The Pearl

LAURENCE STERNE
  A Sentimental Journey
  Tristram Shandy
ROBERT LOUIS STEVENSON
  Kidnapped
  Treasure Island
TOM STOPPARD
  Professional Foul
  Rosencrantz and Guildenstern are Dead
JONATHAN SWIFT
  Gulliver's Travels
JOHN MILLINGTON SYNGE
  The Playboy of the Western World
TENNYSON
  Selected Poems
W. M. THACKERAY
  Vanity Fair
DYLAN THOMAS
  Under Milk Wood
FLORA THOMPSON
  Lark Rise to Candleford
J. R. R. TOLKIEN
  The Hobbit
ANTHONY TROLLOPE
  Barchester Towers
MARK TWAIN
  Huckleberry Finn
  Tom Sawyer
JOHN VANBRUGH
  The Relapse
VIRGIL
  The Aeneid
VOLTAIRE
  Candide
KEITH WATERHOUSE
  Billy Liar
EVELYN WAUGH
  Decline and Fall
JOHN WEBSTER
  The Duchess of Malfi
H. G. WELLS
  The History of Mr Polly
  The Invisible Man
  The War of the Worlds
OSCAR WILDE
  The Importance of Being Earnest
THORNTON WILDER
  Our Town
TENNESSEE WILLIAMS
  The Glass Menagerie
VIRGINIA WOOLF
  Mrs Dalloway
  To the Lighthouse
WILLIAM WORDSWORTH
  Selected Poems
WILLIAM WYCHERLEY
  The Country Wife
W. B. YEATS
  Selected Poems